THE ANTHONY HECHT LECTURES
IN THE HUMANITIES

Second Chances

Shakespeare and Freud

STEPHEN GREENBLATT

ADAM PHILLIPS

Yale UNIVERSITY PRESS

New Haven and London

This book was first presented as the Anthony Hecht Lectures in the Humanities given by Stephen Greenblatt and Adam Phillips at Bard College and the Morgan Library & Museum in 2022. The lectures have been revised for publication.

Published with assistance from the Kingsley Trust Association Publication Fund established by the Scroll and Key Society of Yale College.

Yale University Press books may be purchased in quantity for educational, business, or promotional use. For information, please e-mail sales.press@yale.edu (U.S. office) or sales@yaleup.co.uk (U.K. office).

Set in Minion type by Integrated Publishing Solutions.
Printed in the United States of America.

Library of Congress Control Number: 2023948635
ISBN 978-0-300-27636-7 (hardcover : alk. paper)

A catalogue record for this book is available from the British Library.

This paper meets the requirements of ANSI/NISO Z39.48-1992 (Permanence of Paper).

10 9 8 7 6 5 4 3 2 1

The Anthony Hecht Lectures in the Humanities, given biennially at Bard College, were established to honor the memory of this preeminent American poet by reflecting his lifelong interest in literature, music, the visual arts, and cultural history. Through his poems, scholarship, and teaching, Anthony Hecht has become recognized as one of the moral voices of his generation, and his works have had a profound effect on contemporary American poetry. The books in this series will keep alive the spirit of his work and life.

To Judith Clark and Ramie Targoff

Contents

Second Chances

Introduction

This co-authored investigation of second chances originated in a series of personal questions provoked by reading Adam Phillips's book *On Missing Out: In Praise of the Unlived Life*. The book set me thinking about the shape of my own life, about its division into two geographical halves on opposite sides of the country, and two marriages, and two bouts of childrearing, and even two writing careers, one aimed strictly at academic readers and the other aimed at a more general public. I suggested to Adam that we write a book together. I would write an introduction and then focus on Shakespeare (Chapters 1–4); he would write the chapters on Freud (Chapters 5–7) and the conclusion; and we would collaborate and consult with each other throughout the writing of the separate chapters. By bringing to bear on our subject these two figures on whom we have spent decades of reflection and study, we would stand a chance of clarifying some of the issues at stake in second chances. We would do so not because we write in the same register or with the same points of reference, any more than our authors do, but precisely because we—and they—do not. Our styles of thinking and writing are different, but the differences would give us an opportunity to explore more fully our shared fascination. The project of representation—the work of the playwright—differs from the project of psychoanalysis. A career spent analyzing Shakespeare's plays brings to bear perceptions distinct from those of a career spent analyzing patients. In this project we would each serve as the other's second chance.

What does it all mean? I wondered. I feel I have led two distinct adult lives, as if one story came to an end and I embarked on another. Of course, this is not entirely true. I am well aware that much of my identity, extending even to my choice of profession, was already formed by the time I reached adulthood. "Stevie, put that book down and stop reading," my mother would urge me, "You'll ruin your eyes." "Stevie, the absent-minded professor," my father called me. There are innumerable filaments that tie together the many decades of my existence: tangled memories, family members who reach back to my earliest childhood, friends I have cherished across the years, the steady, unbroken love I bear for my three children, long-term professional engagements as scholar and teacher.

Nonetheless, the feeling remains that I was somehow given a second chance and that my existence has been split in two, a split conveniently marked, after I had graduated from being "Stevie," by a small further change in my name. In the first half of my adult life everyone who knew me at all well called me "Steve"; in the second half I became "Stephen." I did not actively choose to make this change, nor did it result from a ritual or ceremony; it occurred mysteriously, as if it were an occult symbolic recognition that something had happened.

When people now address me as "Steve," I know at once that they are emissaries from my earlier life, one with a distinct set of affections, desires, ambitions, and experiences. The name conjures up a particular house with a view of the Golden

Gate Bridge, biking in the Berkeley hills, backpacking in the Sierras, crowds of protesters in Sproul Plaza, the scent of eucalyptus mingled with tear gas, young colleagues with whom I shared work and argued and laughed. Most of these colleagues will remain forever young in my mind, for once I moved away from California I never saw or heard from most of them again. A complex, intimate network of friendships (and some enmities) fashioned over years almost instantly dissolved, leaving only a few lingering traces. This sense of an ending dovetailed with the painful ending of my marriage. There was no going back.

"Stephen" has for me quite different resonances: an old house on the street where George Washington had his headquarters, the deliberate fashioning of a writing style distinct from the academic one I had long cultivated, hours of committee work helping to bring scholars at risk in different parts of the world to safety at Harvard, a wilderness retreat in Vermont, multiple years spent living in Berlin and in Rome, and, above all, the beloved person with whom I live. If I had lived only one of what seem to me now like two stories—if I had remained "Steve" and never become "Stephen"—would I therefore have known only one of two distinct selves? Would my life have been incomplete or unrealized?

These questions are obviously quite specific to my personal history and depend as such upon a peculiar set of circumstances, including my social class, my profession, and my sex. But Adam Phillips's book served as a helpful reminder that any personal history, however idiosyncratic, is a version of a shared human condition and therefore of a shared set of conundrums. This reminder is one of the virtues of psychoanalysis and has been since its beginnings. In psychoanalysis, after all, you are urged not only to look deeply and unflinchingly into yourself but also to look around and take in the extent to which your particular desires and fears—here the desire and fear provoked by the possibility of either having or missing a second chance in life—are variations on universal themes.

Just how ubiquitous these themes are is apparent in the history of literature, which has long taken as its province alternative or renewed or transformed existences. Innumerable stories explore the realization or failure of second chances, depending upon accident or acts of will or the concatenation of circumstances that we call fate or destiny. Art enables us to rehearse the experience of loss and recovery—to know the joy, as in comedy, that comes with a renewal of love and pleasure, to face the pain, as in tragedy, that comes with realizing that certain forms of damage can never be repaired. It is as if the longing for a second chance were so central to our existence as human beings that we contrive to reproduce that longing again and again in symbolic form. According to the biblical story of the Flood—which has its roots in much older Mesopotamian myths—the entire life of our species is an extended second chance in the aftermath of the Creator's decision to destroy humanity once and for all. Every time we see a rainbow in the sky, we are reminded that continued human existence is contingent on a divine change of mind, a god's decision to grant us a reprieve.

The Flood story turns not on a species-wide reformation; the god in the story is too realistic to expect that from us. Redemption instead depends on one person—Atrahasis in the Sumerian version, Noah in the Hebrew one—whose virtue, energy, and survival instincts save the day. Even if the stakes are collective, second chances taken or missed are almost always stories of particular people. The biblical narratives chronicle the destiny of the whole of God's Chosen People, but the focus is almost entirely on a succession of named individuals whose fate, as in the story of Joseph and his brothers, depends on their specific and highly personal achievement of a second chance.

Christianity brilliantly deployed this narrative strategy in weaving together the Hebrew scriptures with what became known as the New Testament. All of humanity fell as a consequence of the disobedience of Adam and Eve, but redemption—the quintessential second chance—came through the life and the sacrifice of one man. Once again the story depends upon a single hero, Jesus of Nazareth, who undoes the general curse laid upon our entire species and makes it possible for at least some number of us—the faithful—to recover what had seemed irreparably gone. Indeed those so blessed would not merely return to the original state in which the first man and woman had been placed; they would instead enjoy an even better existence. They could find what the poet Milton called "a paradise within thee, happier far" than the physical paradise that humans had lost. And those for whom such inner happiness still seemed very far away could always live in hope for the ultimate second chance, the state of heavenly bliss.[1]

It is not only in the Bible (and its sources) that this basic narrative strategy—a universal interest in second chances explored in the fate of particular individuals—is found. The individual's dream of a second chance does not have to be realized; it may exist only as an alternative, a possible fate. Homer's Achilles is given a choice: he can remain safely at home and live a long, quiet, uneventful life or he can go off to Troy and achieve glory at the cost of an early death. As the *Iliad* unfolds, that uneventful life recedes to a vanishing point, but its theoretical possibility continues to haunt the epic's main action, an action built around the enraged hero's decision to withdraw completely from the war effort. Had Achilles clung to that decision, had he returned to the land from which he sailed, everything would have been different. But, of course, he returns to battle.

In the *Odyssey* this alternative life, the life Achilles could have chosen but did not, still makes its presence felt in the underworld. "There's not a man in the world more blest than you," Odysseus tells the shade of the great warrior; "Time was, when you were alive, we Argives / honored you as a god, and now down here, I see, / you lord it over the dead in all your power." Achilles will have none of it:

> No winning words about death to *me*, shining Odysseus!
> By god, I'd rather slave on earth for another man—
> some dirt-poor tenant farmer who scrapes to keep alive—
> than rule down here over all the breathless dead.

Even after death—especially after death—Achilles fiercely clings to the alternative life he might have led.[2]

It is precisely this alternative life, the life Achilles failed to have, that powerfully resonates in the figure of Odysseus. Odysseus is the embodiment of the dream of a second chance. Not only does he manage to survive the ten-year struggle to conquer Troy and then return to his beloved Ithaca; before his return he spends seven more years in the company of the nymph Calypso. And his survival through many dangers depends upon his gift for inventing and inhabiting imaginary lives. "Any man—any god who met you—would have to be / some champion lying cheat to get past you," Athena says admiringly, "for all-round craft and guile." Even when he manages to kill the suitors who occupy his house and be reunited with his wife and son, he has not, as the poem makes clear, reached an end. He will leave home again, venturing out into new, unexplored territory and living a life that does not resemble anything he has lived before. Odysseus is the king of the perennially renewed and renewable identity.[3]

Why do we call the successive adventures of the "man of many wiles" or even his return to Ithaca a "second chance"? Shouldn't we speak rather of Odysseus's third, fourth, or tenth chance? In some sense this multiplication is obviously correct, as it is with people who marry and divorce and remarry again and again, searching each time for the fulfillment they crave and have failed to find. "Second chance" in such cases is largely a convenient shorthand for repeated effort, as if to say, "Who's counting?" But even for a sprawling epic like the *Odyssey* the term is something more than shorthand. The perennial freshness of the work derives in part from the hero's response to each of his experiences not as a version of what he has already gone through multiple times but rather as a new lease on life, a second chance. It is as if in one's imaginative or emotional life there are not an endless number of chances—as if renewal, however often it has occurred, always feels like a second chance.

That the Bible and the Homeric epics so prominently feature second chances suggests that it is not merely this or that character who explores the possibility of renewing or redoing a life. That possibility is a constituent feature of the literary imagination itself. It is one of the key reasons we are drawn to the whole enterprise and take pleasure in the waking dreams it allows us to enter. We enter the dreams all the more readily because each of us without exception has constant practice in doing so. Literature is an organized, disciplined, and collectively shared extension of the dream life in which we all spend part of every night. And the link to dreams returns us to the psychoanalytic dimension that fascinated Freud and that Adam Phillips has been exploring for decades.

Adam Phillips's book, *Missing Out,* takes off from the recognition that much of our mental life is concerned with needs that are not being met and longings that are not fulfilled. But as its subtitle—*In Praise of the Unlived Life*—suggests, the life we might have lived that never happens may in fact enrich our consciousness and expand our sympathies. And it may do so not despite but precisely because it is unlived. This observation is obviously true of our wildest daydreams, but it is likely to apply as well to more plausible fantasies. It is certainly not the case that our lives are necessarily impoverished by leaving unrealized much that may seem to lie within our grasp.[4]

That said, in some circumstances the dream of a second chance may become so imperative that it compels an attempt to achieve it at any cost. Or rather the alternative to making such an attempt may come to seem unbearable. What is to be done when the prospect of another year in the same place or the same job or the same relationship feels like a prison sentence? How to survive when each day is experienced as a troubled dream from which there is no awakening?

This is hardly only a modern dilemma. In the seventeenth century Milton wrote that an unhappy marriage was like "two carcasses chained unnaturally together." In Genesis 2:18, God said that "it is not good that the man should be alone," and therefore, or so Milton believed, the merciful Creator had instituted marriage to relieve the loneliness of existence. But Milton found that being trapped in a miserable relationship only intensified that loneliness. He felt, he said, like "a living soul bound to a dead corpse." He penned these reflections in his divorce tracts, a succession of impassioned and, for their time, incredibly daring calls for a change in the law, so that a man or a woman trapped in an irreparably unhappy marriage could have the possibility of a second chance. It would be centuries before that possibility was legitimized. In the absence of a change in the divorce laws, most couples were expected to remain together even if love, assuming it had ever existed, had given way to indifference or loathing. It was, Milton wrote, like being in hell.[5]

But the unhappiness, whether in love or in work, does not have to be so dramatically awful to be experienced as unendurable. It can take the form of counting the days, breathing a sigh of relief when another week has passed, feeling a surprising twinge of disappointment when the routine medical examination reveals nothing wrong, and life simply goes on. In such a state, even the most settled arrangements may be ripe for toppling.

All the same, the toppling is invariably difficult, and when it comes, it is almost always painful. Reading Phillips's praise of the unlived life, I found myself asking why radical transformations ever occur in reality and how I had managed, after so much that seemed fixed and unalterable in my own life, to change course in midstream. To what extent was this change of course a matter of chance, arbitrary, accidental, and unearned, and to what extent was I in control? What was I looking to gain, and what were the costs? In choosing to remake so much of my life, if that in fact was what I had done, was I hoping to correct the blunders I had made in the first half of my adult years? If so, was I now destined to make new blunders or to repeat the old ones? Was I really two different persons? Or despite the significant transformations I felt I had undergone, was mine in fact only one life, looked at from different angles but following in the same tracks that had been laid down from the outset by nature and nurture?

Even as I pondered these questions, I was drawn to explore them obliquely through literature. It is not that this turn toward literature served as an escape from a personal confrontation with the possibility of a second life but rather that literature, and especially that branch of literature that tells stories, has always seemed to me the supreme medium for deepening this confrontation. Plays, poems, and novels all offer powerful ways to imagine alternative life histories and to make it possible to enter into them, whether they are eerily close to one's actual circumstances or as wildly removed from them as the lives of Achilles and Hector.

✷

Some of the greatest of these unlived lives—and hence lives
into which I am most inclined to enter imaginatively—are in
Shakespeare. Their enduring power is not because they are notably realistic and still less because they bear any resemblance
to the circumstances of my own existence—far from it. But
they are lives realized with an extraordinary intensity, and they
are launched into situations that seem to test every nuance of
their being. Those situations—the plots of the plays and the ge-
neric expectations Shakespeare at once arouses, challenges, and
fulfills—confer upon each of the characters a distinct and compelling shape.

"In this harsh world draw thy breath in pain," the dying
Hamlet tells Horatio, "To tell my story." Horatio has reached
for the poisoned cup in order to join his beloved friend in
death, but the prince will not permit it. His concern is not Horatio's fate but rather what he calls his own "wounded name."
That name has a sentient life that may be threatened, damaged,
blotted out. The survival of his story is what matters. He needs
someone, as he puts it, to "report me and my cause aright / To
the unsatisfied." But apart from repeating the entire play, what
would such a report look like?[6]

Heeding the injunction, after his friend's voice has been
silenced forever by death, Horatio proposes to give to Fortin-
bras and the entire "unknowing world" an account

> Of carnal, bloody, and unnatural acts,
> Of accidental judgements, casual slaughters,
> Of deaths put on by cunning and forced cause;
> And, in this upshot, purposes mistook
> Fall'n on th' inventors' heads.

A scrupulous thirty-word summary of a formidably complex
plot, but is this what Hamlet meant when he urged his friend

to "tell my story" to the "unsatisfied"? Why did the prince think that his shattered existence, with its baffling, disjointed pieces, could make a coherent narrative? What constituted the shape of a life, one that could be fashioned into a narrative?[7]

Not everyone in Shakespeare's time thought that such fashioning was a worthy goal—or indeed thought that lives had meaningful narrative structures at all. Hamlet's urgent pressure to "tell my story" is essentially alien to the work of his most distinguished contemporary dramatist, Ben Jonson, who repeatedly contrives, even in his most richly plotted plays, to undermine the idea that there is any story to tell. The problem is not, as in *Hamlet*, that there are too many shifting roles but rather something like the reverse. In *Volpone* or *Bartholomew Fair*, Jonson finds fantastically brilliant ways to disclose and unfold traits that are essentially fixed and unchanging. For characters conceived in this way, there is no possibility of a second chance, nor would such a possibility be desirable.

Perfect consistency is for Jonson what most matters— the core of the properly grounded self is steady, fixed, and immutable. A self worthy of respect is hard and polished, indifferent to the constantly shifting impressions of a fickle, unreliable world. Jonson disdains those who read promiscuously and write down whatever strikes them at a particular moment as the truth. Such people have no inner coherence, no stable core of values by which they can measure and judge the world. "What they have discredited and impugned in one week," he tartly observed, "they have before or after extolled the same in another." In doing so they do not reveal their admirable openness to new perspectives but simply their one consistent quality, namely folly. "Such are all the essayists," Jonson writes, disclosing the object of his particular contempt, "even their master Montaigne."[8]

Montaigne was not as far as this dismissal might suggest

from Jonson's sense that each self has a predominant trait and that this trait makes most life stories irrelevant. "There is no one," Montaigne notes, "who, if he listens to himself, does not discover in himself a pattern all his own, a ruling pattern, which struggles against education and against the tempest of the passions that oppose it." But for Montaigne, this ruling pattern— this *forme maistresse,* as he calls it—does not cancel out or even diminish the ceaseless vicissitudes to which he (and everyone else) is subject. These vicissitudes are no mere accidents, set against an enduring substance; they are, Montaigne concludes, what it means to exist:

> I cannot keep my subject still. It goes along befuddled and staggering, with a natural drunkenness. I take it in this condition, just as it is at the moment I give my attention to it. I do not portray being; I portray passing. Not the passing from one age to another, or, as the people say, from seven years to seven years, but from day to day, from minute to minute. My history needs to be adapted to the moment.

A history that must, as Montaigne's late sixteenth-century translator John Florio renders the words, "be fitted to the present" is a history that resists the narrative design of life stories. Hence, Montaigne writes, "even good authors are wrong to insist on fashioning a consistent and solid fabric out of us." Humans are programmatically inconsistent: "We float between different states of mind; we wish nothing freely, nothing absolutely, nothing constantly."[9]

Montaigne was engaged in giving an account of himself. No one has ever done it more magnificently. But his "subject," as he puts it, will not stay still, and his account is deliberately composed without a shape:

> I give my soul now one face, now another, accord-
> ing to which direction I turn it. If I speak of myself
> in different ways, that is because I look at myself in
> different ways.

This sounds at first like a matter of perspective: the angle at which one regards an object, even so intimately familiar an object as oneself, would necessarily change the terms of a depiction. But it is not only a matter of the shifting position of the beholder; rather it is the inner life of the self, as well as the position of the viewer, that is constantly in motion:

> All contradictions may be found in me by some twist
> and in some fashion. Bashful, insolent; chaste, las-
> civious; talkative, taciturn; tough, delicate; clever,
> stupid; surly, affable; lying, truthful; learned, igno-
> rant; liberal, miserly, and prodigal: all this I see in
> myself to some extent according to how I turn; and
> whoever studies himself really attentively finds in
> himself, yes, even in his judgment, this gyration and
> discord.

The essays manifest Montaigne's astonishing determination to keep the recollection of himself entire and hence to remain, as he puts it, alive. But the only way for him to do so is to be, as far as possible, without a fixed and unchanging quality, without a series of determining actions, without a story—completely naked. A life in perpetual gyration and discord, and hence without any narrative coherence or turning point or renewal, is a life without the possibility of a second chance.[10]

Jonson and Montaigne serve as mutually opposing alterna-tives to Shakespeare's vision of life history, to whatever it is that

his characters mean when, like Hamlet, they speak of their lives
as stories and want urgently to tell them or have them told. In
The Tempest, inviting Alonso, the king of Naples, into his cell,
Prospero offers to pass the night

> With such discourse as, I not doubt, shall make it
> Go quickly away: the story of my life,
> And the particular accidents gone by
> Since I came to this isle.

"I long / To hear the story of your life," replies Alonso, "which
must / Take the ear strangely." Prospero here speaks of the events
on the isle as accidents, but these accidents are not (as in Jonson) set against the fixed and stable substance of an unchanging character, and they do not (as in Montaigne) undermine
a coherent narrative. They are rather the constitutive elements
in the plot, the story of how, after making a series of catastrophic
mistakes, Prospero achieved a second chance in life.[11]

By immersing himself in his books and ceding the exercise of power to his treacherous brother, Prospero disastrously
failed as duke of Milan. He botched his first chance. His exile
on the island has been a prolonged waiting period until he can
have a second chance. In *The Tempest* even those events that
seem quintessentially accidental—shipwreck, for example—
are revealed to be part of an overarching design, a design that
brings about the inward transformation that makes a return to
Milan possible.[12] It is not simply that Prospero needs to come
to terms with his own failure and with his brother's perfidy.
The story of Prospero's life centers on a momentous shift in his
moral being from vengeance to forgiveness, a struggle to give
up the daughter over whom he has had sole possession, and a
fateful abjuring of his magical powers.[13]

For Shakespeare, life stories are stories of transformation. He created characters who exist in time and are constrained by it. Anyone can daydream continually about the lives it might be possible to live, but in reality there are only limited opportunities to walk through a door that briefly opens and may never open again. Prospero is intensely aware that the decisive moment has come; he must act upon it now or accept the fact that he will not return to Milan. Thanks to the magic he has mastered through his books, he has been living like a colonial lord, with the slave Caliban to do all the nasty jobs and a nimble servant, Ariel, to do the rest of his bidding. But for Prospero this existence is not a real life; it is a long parenthesis, and he is willing to take whatever risks he must to bring it to an end.

And if he were to fail? *The Tempest* does not engage in such speculation, though the possibility of failure is what gives the plot its urgency. "Burn but his books," Caliban urges his fellow conspirators, and then "thou mayst brain him . . . or with a log / Batter his skull, or paunch him with a stake." At the end of the play Prospero is leaving the island and heading back to Milan to resume his dukedom. If there is something bittersweet about this return—"every third thought shall be my grave," he says—it nonetheless holds out the deeply satisfying prospect of a second chance.[14]

The achievement of a second chance is the crucial difference between the protagonists of Shakespeare's late romances and the protagonists of the tragedies. The former—Pericles, Cymbeline, Leontes, Prospero—recover something that seemed irrecoverable and find a way to begin again; the latter—Hamlet, Othello, Lear, Macbeth, and the other tragic heroes—are haunted by what might have been but are trapped in circumstances from which there is no escape. "The time is out of joint," Hamlet exclaims, "Oh, cursed spite / That ever I was born to set it right." The prince is tormented by the possibility of a life that should have had a different shape. The glorious prospects that made him "Th' expectancy and rose of the fair state,/The glass of fashion and the mold of form" have, by the death of his father, been utterly ruined. Long before the unfolding of the events that will ultimately destroy him and most of those around him, Hamlet understands that he can never restore the time or recover an existence that has been disjointed. His first chance is irrevocably gone, and for him there will be no second chance.[15]

Such is the fate of all of Shakespeare's tragic heroes, however distinct each of them is in circumstance and character. For Shakespeare the essence of tragedy is the absence of a second chance, or, rather, it is this absence conjoined with an unbearably intense, unrealizable desire for one. This desire is aroused not only in the protagonists but in the audience as well. Perhaps the most extreme instance is in *Othello,* whose long performance history includes many accounts of audience members shouting out warnings in a vain attempt to awaken Othello to the trick that is being played on him. Such interventions, hopelessly at odds with the very nature of theater, are an inept tribute to the play's extraordinary ability to provoke an urge to ward off the disaster and give the marriage between the deluded husband and his unjustly accused wife a second chance. But the smothered Desdemona briefly recovers her breath only to die and leave Othello to face what he has done. "Here is my journey's end."[16] A few moments later, before committing suicide, he asks the onlookers to remember that he has done the state some service and to speak of him as he was—or rather as he understands the meaning of his life story.

Virtually all Shakespeare's characters anticipate a future that will bring their story to a close, and at the same time and by virtue of the same narrative exigency they are aware of a past that insistently makes itself felt in the present. Hence the constant tendency in his work—so much in violation of Jonson's aesthetic—to include brilliant flashes from what Prospero terms the "dark backward and abysm of time." Prospero's daughter Miranda has a dreamlike recollection from her early childhood—she was not yet three years old—that she had "four or five women once that tended me." Helena in *A Midsummer Night's Dream* treasures the memory of her intense childhood friendship with Hermia, a friendship that seemed to merge their two selves into a single body:

> As if our hands, our sides, voices, and minds
> Had been incorporate.

Similarly, in *As You Like It,* Celia lovingly describes her long physical and emotional intimacy with Rosalind:

> We still have slept together,
> Rose at an instant, learned, played, eat together,
> And wheresoe'er we went, like Juno's swans
> Still we went coupled and inseparable.[17]

Not all the memories of the past are such happy ones. The duchess of York in *Richard III* conjures up the earliest moments of her wicked son's miserable life—

> A grievous burden was thy birth to me;
> Tetchy and wayward was thy infancy.

—remarking as well on her son's slow rate of growth—

> He was the wretched'st thing when he was young,
> So long a-growing, and so leisurely.

And, in a similar vein, we are offered a glimpse of Coriolanus's childhood, through a description of his small son:

> He's such a confirmed countenance! I saw him run after a gilded butterfly, and when he caught it he let it go again, and after it again, and over and over he comes, and up again, catched it again. Or whether his fall enraged him, or how 'twas, he did so set his teeth and tear it! O, I warrant, how he mammocked it!

Coriolanus's mother, Volumnia, recognizes the trait—"One on's father's moods."[18]

Details like these are telling signs of an urge to construct a coherent life story, a story that charts developments over time, linking the present to the distant past. The significance of these glimpses into the past is not that they are necessarily accurate. During the night in the Athenian woods we learn that the young Helena was not in fact as perfectly "incorporate" with Hermia as her idealized picture suggested. "She was a vixen when she went to school," Helena now remembers, "And though she be but little, she is fierce." So too the aged Justice Shallow in 2 Henry IV loves to dwell on the dashing exploits of his youth, but Falstaff relentlessly pierces his illusions about himself:

> I do remember him at Clement's Inn, like a man made after supper of a cheese paring.

But even if they are not reliable, these memories are always psychologically resonant. Hamlet gives us a tormented glimpse of how his parents' intimacy looked to him when he was a child:

> Must I remember? Why, she would hang on him,
> As if increase of appetite had grown
> By what it fed on.

Was it actually so? Impossible to say, yet we learn from this involuntary memory something deeply important about Hamlet, something that shapes our understanding of his story.[19]

None of these sudden flashbacks—and there are dozens
and dozens of them in Shakespeare's work—is structurally significant. But they serve to convey a sense of what for him a life,
any life, was and hence how he typically went about constructing a convincing character. Shakespeare repeatedly contrives
to suggest a development over time, from Richard's "tetchy" infancy to his bold, quick, resentful, and murderous adulthood;
from Celia's passionate childhood identification with Rosalind
to her willingness as a young woman to rename herself Aliena
and abandon her home in solidarity with her exiled friend; from
Coriolanus's boyhood marked by ardent curiosity and rage at
whatever resists him to the adult's dangerous blend of martial
valor, destructive impatience, and political stupidity.

There is nothing mechanical in this suggested development—certainly no suggestion that all colicky infants become
cunning murderers or that a childhood proclivity for dismem-
bering butterflies inevitably leads to a military career. But the
glimpses extend into the imagined past of these characters a
principle of developmental probability given magnificent expression by Warwick in 2 *Henry IV*:

> There is a history in all men's lives
> Figuring the natures of the times deceased;
> The which observed, a man may prophesy,
> With a near aim, of the main chance of things
> As not yet come to life, who in their seeds
> And weak beginnings lie intreasurèd.
> Such things become the hatch and brood of time.

Warwick is calculating the likelihood that Northumberland
will turn traitor. He is, like a high-stakes gambler, gauging what

he calls "the main chance," and he does this on the basis of his observation of the "times deceased." But he knows that the best he can hope for is a "near aim." After all, the *Henry IV* plays are built around the difficulty of predicting exactly how the central character, Prince Hal, will turn out.[20]

With Hal, as with so many of Shakespeare's characters, an inward disposition already identifiable in early childhood is launched into an existence where survival depends at once on the viability of this disposition and on accommodation to changing conditions. Though the characters are by no means perfectly free, they are aware of their options, and they grapple, as they approach fateful choices, with a range of impulses shaped by their disposition.[21] The choices that they make help to fashion into a lived life whatever opportunities and limits they have inherited by birth and upbringing. So too, if that life turns sour, their choices help determine whether they actually get the second chance for which they long. There is, as Warwick says, "a history in all men's lives," and for a remarkable number of the figures he brought to life, Shakespeare's artistry enables us to grasp the outlines of this history.

The longing for a second chance, bound up with a vision of life history extending back into early childhood, has an obvious resonance with psychoanalysis. For along with many of the greatest poets, dramatists, and novelists, it is Freud and his successors who ventured farthest into the territory of imagined and realized alternative lives. Freud understood that it was in literature that he would find the profoundest explorations of this territory: he drew deeply upon *Oedipus Rex* and *Hamlet,* with their unflinching search into the past and into the structure of the family for the origins of the soul sickness that afflicts the present. But he was trained as a physician and scientist, and he did not regard his overarching goal as the same as a literary artist's.

Though profoundly influenced and informed by literary culture—and Shakespeare was the writer most often quoted by Freud—psychoanalysis was first and foremost a treatment for the disturbances of childhood that recurred in adult life. This treatment, Freud proposed, could provide, through a process of redescription, a second chance for patients suffering from the traumas, fixations, and developmental arrests of their past. As a form of medical therapy it was, uniquely for its time, a cure by language, the medium of literature, but its purpose was not the one advanced over the centuries by the writers of poetry or fiction.

Freud's hope, at least as he initially conceived it, was not merely to understand and to represent and to entertain but to cure. He wanted to make successful second chances actually possible for those whose psychological condition stood in the way of love or work. Nothing in Shakespeare suggests a comparable ambition. To the extent that the playwright explicitly articulates a goal—and he generally seems very reluctant to do so—it is simply to give his audience the repeated experience of pleasure: "A great while ago the world began, / Hey, ho, the wind and the rain," sings the clown at the end of *Twelfth Night*, "But that's all one, our play is done, / And we'll strive to please you every day." Near the end of his career, in the figure of the magician Prospero, Shakespeare seems to articulate a far grander vision for the artist: "Graves at my command / Have waked their sleepers, oped, and let 'em forth / By my so potent art." But the character immediately repudiates this vision—"Deeper than did ever plummet sound / I'll drown my book"—and in the play's epilogue, appealing for applause, he returns to the clown's modest goal: "Gentle breath of yours my sails / Must fill or else my project fails, / Which was to please."[22]

Freud was hardly indifferent to pleasure, but he did not conceive of therapy as a form of entertainment. If he dreamed of waking the dead and letting them forth, it was in the service of unblocking all that impeded a patient's ability to live a ful-filling life. And he discovered, through the new kind of con-versation that was psychoanalysis, that this unblocking often aroused at least as much resistance as pleasure. Individual de-velopment could be both sabotaged by experience and attacked out of fear by the individual who was seeking help. Indeed, his patients, Freud began to realize, were fundamentally ambiva-lent about their own development. They very much wanted the second chances to grow and change on offer in psychoanalysis, but they also feared and resisted these chances. As an object of desire, Freud discovered, a second chance was a mixed bless-ing. The promise of the new was always being waylaid by the allure of the past; there was something almost addictive about the sufferings of childhood.

The literature Freud was drawn to may have represented with great power and subtlety the formative crises that beset his patients, but his question as a doctor was, What, if any-thing, can be done? Though the task of providing a cure proved more difficult than he had originally anticipated, he never com-pletely abandoned it. At a minimum, as he put it in a late essay, he wanted in his therapeutic practice to pave the way for his patients to achieve "a reconciliation with the repressed mate-rial" that manifested itself in their symptoms. That reconcilia-tion might not be the same as a cure, but it could at least bring about "a certain tolerance for the state of being ill."[23]

In this chastened or reduced form Freud's goal may be said to bear a resemblance to Shakespeare's. Freud set about, one might say, to formulate and formalize in the scientific lan-guage of his time the predicaments Shakespeare was exploring in the dramatic rhetoric of the Renaissance theater. But what Shakespeare staged as drama Freud described and treated as pathology. A vast gulf separates their underlying assumptions and their overarching purposes. Still, it is possible to glimpse some shared elements, and not simply because Freud was an avid reader of Shakespeare. "A certain tolerance for the state of being ill" could serve as a plausible description of the net effect of *Hamlet* and *King Lear,* or perhaps even of the far happier *Twelfth Night* and *The Winter's Tale.* For Shakespeare as for Freud, childhood experiences—and in particular the relations between child and mother—were crucial keys to understanding adult behavior. And like Freud, Shakespeare was fascinated by the ways in which some individuals, shaped by these childhood experiences, made catastrophic choices, persuading themselves that they had no alternatives, while others found ways to recover what seemed irrevocably lost. No human, in Shakespeare's view, leads a perfectly charmed life, a life without frustration, fear, mistakes, and the intimation of despair. The comedies are almost as full of misery and loss as the tragedies. The question is how, in the face of inevitable folly and woe, some characters find a way to tolerate, even embrace, the human condition.

For Freud the question was not merely how people—his contemporaries in fin-de-siècle Vienna—managed to survive amid the very real hardships of their lives but how they managed to sustain the enjoyment that made life worth living. It would be part of Freud's contribution to modern thought to show us how people had found ingenious ways of getting pleasure from their suffering. While religion had once been the sustaining drama of most lives, now there were, in his view, forms of sexuality and violence largely freed from theological trappings and deeply rooted in the structure of the family and of society. In an outpouring of case studies, theoretical papers, and speculative essays, Freud analyzed the behavior of men and women who were often driven to wild extremes, whether of tyranny or abjection, asceticism or libidinousness, self-love or self-loathing,

in their search for forms of happiness—second chances—that
they at the same time fiercely resisted.

There are moments in Shakespeare's work that echo a
Freudian diagnosis of civilization and its discontents:

> Man, proud man,
> Dress'd in a little brief authority,
> Most ignorant of what he's most assured—
> His glassy essence—like an angry ape
> Plays such fantastic tricks before high heaven
> As makes the angels weep; who, with our spleens,
> Would all themselves laugh mortal.[24]

But, of course, this is not the playwright speaking; it is one of
his characters, and a highly flawed one at that. Shakespeare's
work took the form of stories. Through these stories, he imagined his way deeply into the longing for a second chance and
into the obstacles, both internal and external, that stood in the
way of fulfilling this longing. As far as is known, however, the
playwright never attempted to reflect in a more conceptual
way on what he had discovered. It was Freud who initiated the
sustained modern attempt to describe in more theoretical and
analytical terms the urgent desire to have a second chance.
And he did so not, or not only, in the hope of enhancing understanding but in the hope of enhancing health.

The Freudian diagnosis was that people suffer from what
they do not want to know about themselves, and what they do
not want to know about themselves is the range and intensity
of their unacceptable desires, desires that their societies can neither gratify nor even allow them to recognize. The attempted
self-cure for how unaware—how unconscious—of ourselves our
societies need us to be is a consoling, grandiose picture of ourselves as omnipotent and omniscient. In reality, Freud thought,

our condition is far closer to helplessness, in relation both to our daunting internal world of instinctual desire and to a persecutory external world of political and economic hardship. This helplessness prompts wildly unrealistic and destructive cravings for power and autonomy. The second chance Freud offered with psychoanalysis was a more realistic, and therefore potentially more satisfying, apprehension of what he took to be our true nature: the second chance of not living as a wishful, and therefore permanently enraged and vengeful, fantasist.

The second chances that Shakespeare dramatized and Freud diagnosed and tried to treat were inevitably the second chances of their times; what might have looked like first chances in seventeenth-century Britain would be quite different from the first chances available in turn-of-the-century Vienna. And yet, of course, neither Shakespeare nor Freud can avoid talking about the discrepancy, the incongruity people feel between the lives they have, whatever those lives are, and the lives they want. For Freud and his modern patients the question was, What is stopping them from getting the lives they want? As Freud addressed this question, he extended it into an inquiry about where his patients' ideas of a good and desirable life came from, of how their beliefs about satisfaction and meaning fitted into their personal histories. Freud, as a modern medical doctor, was in the business of finding useful and convincing solutions and explanations—explanations as solutions—for the sufferings of his patients. If this proffered cure seemed like a secularized version of redemption, it was significantly less ambitious and magical than the redemption on offer in religion: psychoanalysis has never had any truck with the supernatural. As Freud famously once put it, the aim of psychoanalytic treatment was to turn hysterical misery into common human unhappiness. So where Freud explains, we might say, Shakespeare dramatizes; where

Freud wants to interrupt, or disrupt, or put a stop to a drama of human suffering, Shakespeare wants to show us what it might be to see it all the way through. And where Shakespeare shows us the completed actions of his dramas—to bring us to the final act and the closing appeal for applause—Freud describes the unavoidably uncompleted actions of his treatments and his theories.

Though it is tempting to think of Freud as bringing up to the surface what was only implicit and hidden in Shakespeare— hidden, that is, even to the artist himself—I think that Shakespeare was highly conscious of these issues. Throughout his career he constantly doubled back on stories he had already told, as if to give them a new lease on life. The enemy brothers in *As You Like It*, Oliver and Orlando, are mirrored in Claudius and Old Hamlet and again in Leontes and his sworn brother Polixenes. Each of these returns functions as a theatrical second chance, just as each of the characters in the doubled pairs embodies the unrealized possibility, the unlived life, of the other. For that matter, since virtually all these stories were borrowed from one or more other writers, each of them in Shakespeare's version is already experiencing a second chance. Hence the separated twins in Plautus's *Menaechmi* return in *The Comedy of Errors,* accompanied now by two twin servants. Giraldi Cintho's nasty little tale of the Moorish captain tricked by his wicked ensign into murdering his Venetian wife is given a spectacular refashioning as *Othello* and then, years later, is told again, this time without the ensign, in *The Winter's Tale,* a play that is itself a refashioning of Robert Greene's *Pandosto.* So too the possessive old king who dreams of whiling away years in prison with his beloved daughter Cordelia returns in *The Tempest* as the possessive old duke on the ocean island with his beloved daughter Miranda.

All these doublings and variations, moreover, take place

within a medium that is the embodiment of the idea of the second chance. As actor, entrepreneur, and playwright, Shakespeare understood that after the opening day, there could be no simple repetition. Each live performance was different, sometimes in subtle, sometimes in drastic ways. The audience that was alive with excitement on one day would be dead on the next; the actors who seemed listless and confused would discover powers they never knew they possessed; lines that yesterday brought everyone to tears—"O mother, mother! / What have you done"—today produced laughter.[25] And these types of second chances, fulfilling or frustrating, do not even begin to address the inexhaustible variability of live theater. Actors fell ill or left the troupe in the middle of a run; revivals were performed with a completely different cast; plays taken on tour were drastically rewritten to accommodate the smaller number of actors and a different play space; court performances were staged in the presence of the monarch. Nothing stayed the same. And unlike his contemporary Ben Jonson, Shakespeare seems to have accepted and even embraced this radical instability. Most of his scripts are too long to be easily performed in what in the prologue to *Romeo and Juliet* he called the "two hours' traffic of our stage."[26] (Try to read *Hamlet* aloud in only two hours, even without all the exits and entrances, the eerie silences, the dumb show, and the sword fight.) This length probably indicates that Shakespeare expected that with each revival or tour a theater company would pick and choose and in effect give the play a new form.

All this means that Shakespeare reflected deeply, not in an abstract way but at the very heart of his practice, on what it means to have a second chance. It was certainly possible to resist this feature of the medium of the theater. By means of stage directions and other instructions, Shakespeare's colleague Ben Jonson tried, as far as he was able, to fix the performance

of each of his plays into the form he most desired. But Shakespeare showed little sign of such desire. The stage directions
included in his manuscripts, as far as we can tell, were a bare
minimum, and unlike Jonson he seems not to have interested
himself in establishing the final authorial text of his works. For
the most part, as actors know, he leaves them a remarkable
latitude to renew the plays by reimagining them, as he himself
seems to have been prone to reimagine them.

Shakespeare is the supreme virtuoso of the second chance.
Freud is its supreme interpreter. To bring them together as we
have done in this book is an opportunity to read Shakespeare
in the light of Freud and Freud in the light of Shakespeare.
And for the two of us, as for any reader who is in search of
renewal, it is an opportunity to be guided by both the greatest
literary and the greatest psychoanalytic explorer of the second
chance.

1

Shakespeare's First Chance

A fter I went off to university and even later, after I had married and taken my first job and moved three thousand miles away to California, I repeatedly had the same experience: I would return home to see my parents and discover that nothing whatsoever had changed. The modest two-family New England house in which I had grown up, shoehorned in between a large apartment house on one side and a convent school on the other, was as if frozen in time. Neither my parents nor my Aunt Rose, who lived upstairs, had altered a thing: the dark mahogany tables and chairs, the lamps with their bases of Chinese porcelain, the secretary desk with the hidden drawers, the twelve heavy leather-bound volumes of *The Jewish Encyclopedia* in the bookcase in the hall, the little knickknacks on the shelves in the breakfast nook with the yellow wallpaper—all were seemingly untouched. Well, they must in fact have been touched, if only to dust and polish, for everything was perfectly clean and respectable and well kept. There was not a trace of neglect, only a complete indifference to the passage of time. Evidently my parents and my aunt had settled on what they wanted—probably, as far as I could tell, in the mid-1950s—and left it at that.

The inhabitants looked to me as unchanged as the furni-
ture. My father's hair was still largely black (his friends teased
him that he must use shoe polish); my mother and aunt had
long ago fixed upon their chosen hair color and style, which
they maintained impeccably. Their routines, their topics of conversation, and even their ailments remained the same. Every
morning my father walked a half-mile down the hill to take
the trolley to his office on State Street in Boston, where he had
practiced law for some sixty years. On my visits home I would
immediately resume the ritual I had observed from the day I
got my driver's license at the age of sixteen and would drive
down to the trolley stop to pick him up at the end of the day.
Sitting in the car, double-parked, I would watch him jauntily
descend from the T, with his battered briefcase and his fedora
and a smile of recognition when he spotted me. It was as if I
were still a junior in high school.

On these returns I slept in the same bed I had slept in
since I was young, and in the same small room with the imita-
tion wainscoting. The books on the shelves were the same ones
I had loved as a child: *Treasure Island,* a tattered copy of *1001
Nights,* Richard Halliburton's *Book of Marvels,* Pat Frank's Cold
War thriller *Forbidden Area.* When I awoke in the morning,
the crows cawing outside my window sounded like they had
agreed to keep up the identical racket that they had made decades earlier, just to reassure me that nothing whatsoever had
changed. I found it all comforting and at the same time a bit
disquieting.

I am, of course, describing what it means to reenter a
perfectly familiar world, and there is nothing uncanny about
that. The peculiar disquiet I felt had to do with all the changes
within me that were now in sharp contrast to this continuity.
I had gone off to college (as neither of my parents had done); I

had lived in Europe (as no one in my family had done); I had, in the prevailing spirit of the late 1960s and early 1970s, changed my hair and my glasses and my style of dress and my politics and my sense of self.

I realize now, looking back at that time, that I was completely oblivious to all that was in fact changing at home beneath the veneer of sameness. I failed to notice any of the more subtle marks of aging in my parents' faces or in the way that they moved. I did not grasp, let alone honor, their painful effort to comprehend the antiwar movement or the sexual revolution or feminism or the loud music or any of the other exotic fruits that their son was bringing home from his new life in Berkeley, three thousand miles away. In the personal and generational narcissism of that moment, I noticed only my own metamorphosis and what I took to be the monumental immobility of those whom I had left behind.

There was one other thing that I noticed: no sooner was I home than, wearing the trappings of my new identity, I fell back emotionally into all the old ways. I would immediately get on a high horse, as if I possessed a special insight about life; I would feel irrationally enraged at my parents for what I grasped even at the time were things of no importance; I would engage in political arguments that could not possibly lead anywhere. It was as if I were just hitting puberty again. I knew that I was behaving absurdly, but I couldn't stop myself, or if I did for a moment pause, feel ashamed, and act lovingly, I would quickly succumb once again.

It was only after things irreparably fell apart—my father had a sudden heart attack and died after two weeks in the hospital, my aunt Rose was found dead one morning on the bedroom floor upstairs, my mother, bereft of the two mainstays of her life, moved to a small apartment—that I realized that my experience of returning to the past, the recovery that I had found so peculiar, was the stuff of comedy, and specifically of Shakespearean comedy.

Characters in Shakespeare's comedies often want—sometimes desperately—to return to families and to restore relationships that they thought they had lost forever. They long to recover the objects of their desire intact and exactly as they had been forced to leave them, frequently many years earlier. The longing seems hopeless and the prospect of recovery impossible, as they themselves understand. "I to the world am like a drop of water / That in the world seeks another drop," says Antipholus of Syracuse in *The Comedy of Errors*, one of Shakespeare's early plays,

> Who, falling there to find his fellow forth,
> Unseen, inquisitive, confounds himself.
> So I, to find a mother and a brother,
> In quest of them, unhappy, lose myself.

However much they may seem identical, it is not just any water drop that this character seeks to find; it is the one that is unique, irreplaceable, and entirely his own. That is the essence of family: from a sufficient sociological distance all may seem generically alike and mutually interchangeable, but your family is specifically yours.[1]

The plot of *The Comedy of Errors*, lifted directly from a comedy by the Roman playwright Plautus, contrives at once to test and to intensify this sense of unsubstitutable specificity. The situation, which is set out in the opening scene, goes as follows: When the ship on which his family was voyaging split apart during a violent storm, a child was saved by his father but separated from his mother and his identical twin brother. The father settled in Syracuse, where he raised his son, whom, in an act of remembrance, he called Antipholus, the name of the child he had lost at sea. At eighteen Antipholus became intensely inquisitive about his brother and received his father's permission to go off in search of him. In the course of this search, which as the play opens is now in its seventh year, he has been accompanied—a twist added by Shakespeare to the ancient story—by Dromio, one of a pair of identical (and identically named) twin slaves, whom the parents had purchased to serve their sons and who were likewise separated in the storm. In a further twist, Antipholus's father, becoming increasingly anxious as the years pass, has gone off in search of the son who went in search of his brother. The search has taken both father and son, unbeknownst to each other, to Ephesus. There, after a string of mistaken identities and much mad confusion, everything by the play's end is resolved with the whole family happily reunited.

A displaced person, torn away from his or her origins, searches for and finally recovers familial bonds that restore a lost identity. The situation was one to which Shakespeare's imagination returned again and again, as if it were at once a surefire plot device and a recurrent personal fantasy. In some versions of the story, the character has gone in search of what he is fully aware that he has lost; in other versions, the character is unaware of his actual roots and is taken by surprise when those roots are revealed. *The Comedy of Errors* manages to include both types: Antipholus of Syracuse is actively looking for his lost mother and brother, but his twin, Antipholus of Ephesus, has no idea of his true origins and is looking for nothing more than an agreeable rendezvous with his mistress and a quiet lunch with his wife. By the play's end, Antipholus of Syracuse has fulfilled a quest that had seemed impossible; Antipholus of Ephesus has discovered a brother he did not know he had. Both have found their missing father and mother and thereby found themselves as well, retrieving the birth identities they lost in the shipwreck. Against all odds, they have returned to their origins and recovered their first chance.

Shakespeare's prime locus of this recovery, the family, is not something his characters actively choose, any more than any of us initially choose our name or our nationality, our mother tongue or our religion. We are thrown into our families willy-nilly, and with them our particular place and time, our social class, and our range of expectations. Most of us live more or less comfortably for the whole of our lives within this inherited framework of identity. But on occasion the structure can be suddenly and radically altered—Shakespeare's recurrent image for this alteration is shipwreck. Some of the victims of shipwreck are haunted by their loss; others are ignorant of it. But the original circumstances always hover somewhere in the background as the all-important first chance, and Shakespeare loves to represent its blissful, wonder-working resurrection.

In one of his last plays, *Pericles, Prince of Tyre,* Shakespeare stages a recovery strikingly similar to the one he depicted in the early *Comedy of Errors.* On a sea voyage Pericles' wife, Thaisa, died in childbirth during a violent storm; grief-stricken he put her body in a coffin and consigned it to a watery grave. But it turns out that she was not dead, only unconscious. Washed ashore in her coffin and revived by a mysterious gentleman learned in the healing arts, she has spent her years as a priestess in the temple of Diana. At the play's climax she is reunited first with her husband and then her daughter: "Look who kneels here," Pericles declares, directing the gaze of his wife to their daughter, whom he has also just recovered: "Flesh of thy flesh, Thaisa, / Thy burden at the sea, and called Marina."[2]

Only a moment or so earlier Marina, her virginity on offer as a commodity for purchase by the highest bidder, was lamenting the loss of her first chance:

> My derivation was from ancestors
> Who stood equivalent with mighty kings.
> But time hath rooted out my parentage,
> And to the world and awkward casualties
> Bound me in servitude.

Now suddenly, her virginity still intact, she has regained the exalted social status that came with the family that has been so miraculously resurrected.[3]

In a similar vein, Miranda in *The Tempest* is asked by her father, Prospero, if she can remember anything from "the dark backward and abysm of time," before they were shipwrecked on the remote ocean island. Her distant memory of class privilege—the servants who once tended to her—is the key to the girl's original and true identity, an identity displaced and forgotten when her father was deposed. By the play's end, now betrothed to a prince, Miranda is poised to return to the social rank to which she was born, the rank in which she once had and now will again have four or five women constantly attending her.[4]

So too in yet another late play, *Cymbeline,* Guiderius and Arviragus—kidnapped as infants and brought up in a cave—eventually learn that they are the sons of the British king. Once again the revelation marks a return to a primordial identity that had never been completely lost. Even their kidnapper, whom the boys call father, remarks to himself with wonder the extent to which their origin, the royal family into which they were born, continues to exercise a shaping power over their natures:

> 'Tis wonder
> That an invisible instinct should frame them
> To royalty unlearned, honor untaught,

> Civility not seen from other, valor
> That wildly grows in them, but yields a crop
> As if it had been sowed.

At the play's end the kidnapper returns the boys to their father, King Cymbeline, who is understandably wary of imposture—after all, he has not seen his sons, two strapping young men, since their infancy—and seeks some proof. On his neck, he recalls, the infant Guiderius had "a mole, a sanguine star; / It was a mark of wonder." "This is he," the kidnapper replies, "Who hath upon him still that natural stamp." Reassured by this piece of forensic evidence, the king gives way to an extravagant burst of joy: "Ne'er mother / Rejoiced deliverance more." It is as if time had been turned back to the moment of their birth. As Cymbeline makes clear, the young men have recovered their first chance, the circle or orbit that was meant to be their natural sphere:

> Blest pray you be,
> That, after this strange starting from your orbs,
> You may reign in them now![5]

These semi-magical restorations of social status, typical of the ancient literary romance genre upon which Shakespeare was drawing, imply that rank and class are natural givens, like eye color or skin pigment. The genre's popularity reflects the fact that Shakespeare and his contemporaries had an intensely strong sense of what they called blood, particularly if any property—whether a grand estate of seventy-five thousand acres or a few pewter spoons—was involved. Hence when characters recover their birth families, even after a gap of many years, they are felt to recover their original identity—the truth of their blood—along with whatever appropriately goes with it.

However quaint or reactionary this Renaissance notion now seems to us, we in fact have a strong version of it in genetic inheritance, a notion that in certain circumstances, such as paternity lawsuits, can result in a comparable restitution of status and property. Our own reflections on what *Cymbeline* calls the signs of "invisible instinct," regardless of upbringing, lead us back to innate personality traits inherited at birth. The key point is that in Shakespeare the recovery of the birth family, even by a character who has had little or no experience of that family, is a recovery of the identity conferred by the first chance.

We do not ordinarily recognize our birth family as a chance at all. Like our genetic inheritance, like the infinitely complex set of random accidents that issued in our coming to exist, it is simply what is. The circumstances into which we are born are what we have been dealt as our lot (though perhaps we should note that a "lot" is a kind of chance, as in lottery). We can subsequently be adopted; we can be kidnapped as infants and raised by someone else; we can be shipwrecked and wash up on another shore; we can run away and attach ourselves to surrogate families. But at least as Shakespeare conceived it, these are all second chances, even if the first one was brief or unhappy.

It is only when what we have been dealt has been lost—stolen from us, discarded, decisively rejected, gone missing, vanished, or simply died—that we see it clearly in retrospect as our first chance, "first" precisely because it is over and will not come back. But the pleasure of Shakespeare's comedies has to do with having it come back. The characters recover what seemed irrecoverable, and we are invited to share the thrill of this recovery. In near-miraculous renewals of what was lost, we not only get our first chance back but also get to be conscious of it. We discover the joy and wonder of relationships that might otherwise have been entirely taken for granted.

Let us return for a moment to our paradigmatic example of *The Comedy of Errors*. The wife who has lost her husband and her two babies becomes a nun and eventually an abbess. Years pass. Then by a series of mad accidents, the whole family (slaves included) is reunited. In a strange and resonant metaphor (one Shakespeare remembered and reused in *Cymbeline*) the mother expresses her astonishment at the sudden recovery of her lost boys:

> Thirty-three years have I but gone in travail
> Of you, my sons, and till this present hour
> My heavy burden ne'er delivered.

She has been in labor for more than three decades, and only now, finally, she has given birth. It is a deliberately mad image, one meant to call attention to the impossibility of what the festive comedy is allowing us to experience. She invites everyone to what she calls "a gossips' feast," that is, to the traditional celebration of a christening. As the play ends, the born-again family, along with two slaves and the city's ruler, goes off to partake in this perfect emblem of the recovered first chance.[6]

After years in suspension, family life has miraculously resumed, as if it had been able to return to the point where it had left off. It was just such a resumption that I felt I was experiencing—in my case, in frustration—when I returned home and had the illusion that nothing had changed. The final act of *The Comedy of Errors* does not altogether leave the illusion unchallenged. The father, seeing his son after a gap of seven years, is dismayed that the child he lovingly reared does not recognize him. "Grief hath changed me since you saw me last," he grants, "And careful hours with Time's deformèd hand / Have written strange defeatures in my face." But surely, he asks, his son must still recognize his voice? When this too fails, the

father is forced to acknowledge the full force of time's passage
and with it the definitive vanishing of the first chance:

> Not know my voice! O time's extremity,
> Hast thou so cracked and splitted my poor tongue
> In seven short years that here my only son
> Knows not my feeble key of untuned cares?

Perhaps, he reflects poignantly, it is different for parents and
children. The child can forget his parent, but the parent can
never, even in extremis, forget the face or voice of his child:

> Though now this grainèd face of mine be hid
> In sap-consuming winter's drizzled snow,
> And all the conduits of my blood froze up,
> Yet hath my night of life some memory;
> My wasting lamps some fading glimmer left;
> My dull deaf ears a little use to hear.
> All these old witnesses, I cannot err,
> Tell me thou art my son.[7]

These words would be lachrymose proof that time can
never be reversed and that the first chance exists only in the
memory of the old, were it not for the fact that it is all a mistake. The father's reproaches and laments are entirely unneces-
sary. The young man whom he addresses is not the son he
raised but the identical twin whom he has not seen since infancy. That twin has every reason to say flatly, and to the best
of his knowledge truthfully, "I never saw my father in my life."
By contrast, a few minutes later the other son, though he has
been voyaging for seven years, has no difficulty at all recognizing his father. The seeming callousness and the terrible grief it
provokes are simply part of the comedy of errors. There is no

need then for a reckoning or a coming to terms with either moral failure or the cruel passage of time. Instead the story sweeps on to its happy vision of the complete recovery of everything that seemed lost—"That is the chain, sir, which you had of me"; "This purse of ducats I received from you"; "Sir, I must have that diamond from you"; "Thy father hath his life"—culminating in his family's rebirth: "After so long grief such nativity!"[8]

There is, Shakespeare perfectly understood, something artificial, almost absurd, about such fantasies of complete recovery. If you are very lucky, you can sometimes get back a lost gold chain or a purse of ducats, but in your intimate relationships once you have lost the first chance, it almost never returns. The dream of simply reentering the past and picking up where you left off—the slightly queasy dream I had for years whenever I returned home and failed to notice how much had changed forever—is a fragile and evanescent illusion. Illusion, however, is at the center of Shakespeare's comic art, and his artistic medium, the theater, specializes in constantly renewing what seems over. As if in tribute to the power of the imagination to alter the ordinary rules of life, Shakespeare repeatedly embraces and heightens the sense of artifice. "Prove true, imagination, oh, prove true," the heroine of *Twelfth Night* prays, hoping that her brother, presumed drowned, is still alive, and throughout the comedies this prayer, in various forms, is answered.[9]

The birth family is not the sole instance, as Shakespeare conceived it, of comedy's magical recovery, if only as delicious illusion, of the first chance. The other great instance is falling in love. The two, of course, are very different. Falling in love, unlike being born, seems to involve personal agency. A first chance in love, however absolute and unchosen it feels, is therefore never quite a true first chance. It always includes an implicit element of choice based upon a past, upon previous encounters of varying intensity that anticipate and prepare the way and condition one's judgment. And it always reaches back, as Shakespeare understood, to childhood, to the love of one's parents or nurse or tutor. "You have begot me, bred me, loved me," Cordelia tells her father in *King Lear,* "I return those duties back as are right fit." Then she adds a crucial qualification: "When I shall wed, / That lord whose hand must take my plight shall carry / Half my love with him, half my care and duty." Yet this transfer of familial love, partial or entire, is not how the experience of love is depicted in Shakespeare's comedies. Shakespeare treats birth and love as strikingly similar in their shared sense of sudden, unwilled, radical initiation.[10]

In *As You Like It* Rosalind and Orlando merely exchange banalities at a wrestling match—

> ROSALIND. Young man, have you challenged
> Charles the wrestler?
> ORLANDO. No, fair princess. He is the general
> challenger. I come but in, as others do, to try with
> him the strength of my youth.

—and they are already deeply in love. Orlando can barely speak: "What passion hangs these weights upon my tongue?" And though Rosalind is never at a loss for words, she is as far gone. Later in the play, in one of Shakespeare's few explicit allusions to a contemporary poet, another character who has fallen madly in love quotes a famous line from Christopher Marlowe: "Who ever loved that loved not at first sight?"[11]

So too Olivia in *Twelfth Night* needs to exchange only a few words with Viola—in her disguise as Cesario—to fall instantly in love with the person she sees:

> How now?
> Even so quickly may one catch the plague?

Methinks I feel this youth's perfections
With an invisible and subtle stealth
To creep in at mine eyes.

And in *The Tempest,* Ferdinand and Miranda do not even need words: "At the first sight," remarks Prospero, "They have changed eyes." They are, he observes with satisfaction, "both in either's powers."[12]

Shakespeare always touches these experiences of falling madly in love with a certain irony. Orlando is mocked for writing execrable poems in praise of Rosalind; Olivia's irresistible Cesario is not what "he" appears to be; Miranda's "thing divine" is simply the first person apart from her father and Caliban she has seen. Even Romeo's passion is framed by Mercutio's ridicule:

Romeo! Humors! Madman! Passion! Lover!
Appear thou in the likeness of a sigh;
Speak but one rhyme, and I am satisfied;
Cry but "Ay me!"

As if on cue, a few moments later, with Romeo sighing, "Oh, that I were a glove upon that hand / That I might touch that cheek!," Juliet on the balcony above cries, "Ay me!"[13]

And yet the mockery does not deflate the romantic ardor, certainly not in *Romeo and Juliet* and not even in the most light-hearted comedies. True, there is something ridiculous in these raptures, as Shakespeare makes most gleefully apparent in *Love's Labour's Lost* and *A Midsummer Night's Dream.* But all of the characters, from the king of Navarre and his three attendant gentlemen to the four young lovers in the Athenian woods, are in the grip of a love that has no precedent in their lives. And this sense of a love that is (or in any case feels like) a first chance confers upon their experience a kind of freshness, a pure singularity, that resists ironic deflation.

Shakespeare repeatedly challenges this singularity, as he does when Prospero responds to Miranda's breathless "O brave new world" by observing wryly, "'Tis new to thee." So too in response to Orlando's case of love-sickness, Rosalind replies with droll reassurance:

> The poor world is almost six thousand years old, and in all this time there was not any man died in his own person, *videlicet* in a love cause. Troilus had his brains dashed out with a Grecian club; yet he did what he could to die before, and he is one of the patterns of love. Leander, he would have lived many a fair year though Hero had turned nun, if it had not been for a hot midsummer night; for, good youth, he went but forth to wash him in the Hellespont and, being taken with the cramp, was drowned, and the foolish chroniclers of that age found it was Hero of Sestos. But these are all lies: men have died from time to time, and worms have eaten them, but not for love.

But this deflationary exercise is part of one of Shakespeare's great courtship scenes, at the end of which, as she tells her cousin, Rosalind is more madly in love than ever: "O coz, coz, coz, my pretty little coz, that thou didst know how many fathom deep I am in love! But it cannot be sounded: my affection hath an unknown bottom, like the Bay of Portugal."[14]

The intensity of romantic love—the feeling that this person, and this person alone, is the fulfillment of your deepest desires, the embodiment of everything you have ever dreamed of possessing, your unique vision of limitless perfection—burns away all previous emotional encounters, all anticipations and rehearsals, all other chances. The plays make it clear that there is always a history of earlier attachments, passions, shared intimacies with friends and family. Moments before Romeo encounters Juliet, he has been mooning over someone else. But the overwhelming feeling that his love is unique, unprecedented, once and for all produces in Romeo, as it does in every other lover in Shakespeare (and, as I can testify, in life), the sense that this experience is a first chance. All those around you can be as ironic as they wish, but you can say, with Romeo, "He jests at scars that never felt a wound."[15] Even the claims of the birth family, the most undeniable of first chances, fade in importance. The comedies repeatedly stage the triumph of romantic passion over all competing considerations, including those of the parents.

In *A Midsummer Night's Dream* the angry father Egeus comes before the duke of Athens to demand that his daughter Hermia marry Demetrius, the man he has chosen for her. But Hermia refuses to obey. She is passionately in love with Lysander, and he with her. "You have her father's love," Lysander tells Demetrius, "Let me have Hermia's. Do you marry him."[16] Besides, Demetrius may claim that he loves Hermia, but he had earlier wooed Helena, who continues to be passionately in love with him. What parents or the state command is irrelevant; what matters are the imperatives of love.

After the lovers have run away, the magical powers of the fairies who inhabit the Athenian woods manage to sort out the relationships, but not before the relationships have been jumbled further in zany confusion and enmity. Once the closest of friends, Hermia and Helena fall out bitterly, and Lysander and Demetrius come to blows. Eventually, the fairies succeed in returning the four young people to their mutual friendship and their original desires. Indeed, true to the idea of the first chance, the lovers resume the bonds they had formed before the play begins. Once again in love with Helena, Demetrius seems to have forgotten that he ever shifted his love to Hermia. The fairies' magical love juice applied to the correct eyes undoes the sadness, anger, and disillusionment that the lovers have known during their frenzied night in the woods, emotions that are the ordinary companions of the loss of a first chance. In *A Midsummer Night's Dream,* as in *The Comedy of Errors,* there is no final reckoning to pay. "These things seem small and undistinguishable," says one of the lovers, awakening out of a drugged sleep, "Like far-off mountains turnèd into clouds." "Methinks I see these things with parted eye," agrees another, "When everything seems double." The betrayal and loss that they have all experienced are forgotten.[17]

A comparable forgetting resolves the problem of the competing claims of the birth family—here the father's angry insistence that his daughter marry the man he has chosen for her. "To you your father should be as a god," the duke had told Hermia, confirming what he calls "the ancient privilege of Athens." The privilege would not have seemed absurd to an Elizabethan audience. Parents in Shakespeare's England did not possess the absolute authority claimed by Egeus—"I may dispose of her, / Which shall be either to this gentleman / Or to her death, according to our law"—but they exercised an overwhelming determining influence on the marriage choices of their children. And the truth is that even now, when this influence has considerably waned, parents continue to shape these choices in subtle and not so subtle ways. But in Shakespeare's comedy, whatever the angry father says, it is desire that has the preeminent right over the authority of the family. By the play's end parental power is simply overruled and forgotten. Romantic love wins.[18]

The birth family as first chance and romantic love as first chance do not always have to conflict, as they do in *A Mid-*

summer Night's Dream. Out of nowhere, at the end of *As You Like It,* the play introduces Hymen, the pagan god of marriage, both to bring the lovers together in marriage and to restore the daughter to her father, the exiled duke. "To you I give myself," Rosalind says to her father, "for I am yours." "To you I give myself," she then says, turning to her lover Orlando, "for I am yours." For a blissful moment the painful feelings that mark the end of one form of first chance and the beginning of another are swept away in what Hymen calls atonement, that is, at-one-ment:

> Then is there mirth in heaven
> When earthly things, made even,
> Atone together.

Immediately in the wake of this spectacle of heavenly unity, word is brought that the duke's wicked brother, miraculously converted by a chance encounter with a religious ascetic, has returned the crown he had usurped. Everything is set to rights, not only for the exiled duke and his daughter Rosalind but also for his followers: "And all their lands restored to them again / That were with him exiled."[19]

The general restoration returns everything to the way it began, as if that were simply how things were meant to be—the first chance is not so much earned as given by the nature of things. There is therefore no need for reflection: the duke does not have to work through his brother's hatred and betrayal, any more than the lovers in *A Midsummer Night's Dream* have to work through the significance of their night in the woods or remember that their relationships had fallen apart. If the characters had to think about such things, they would feel a certain gnawing discomfort, as if they had not actually recovered the first chance at all. The discomfort is figured in *As You Like It* by the play's most thoughtful character, the melancholy Jaques, who is the only character who refuses the restoration at the end, choosing instead to remain in the forest.

A personality inclined toward "thinking too precisely on the event," as Hamlet characterizes himself, would be ill suited for the happy endings of these plays. In *Twelfth Night,* Viola and Sebastian, twin brother and sister, have been separated by a storm at sea; each fears that the other has drowned. When they are finally reunited, Viola is dressed in men's clothes, and their uncanny family resemblance perplexes poor Sebastian, who in truth does not seem like the brightest candle. "Do I stand there?" he asks, staring at his sister in wonder:

> I never had a brother.
> . . . .
> Of charity, what kin are you to me?
> What countryman? What name? What parentage?

What follows is a slow-motion reconstruction of the lost kinship:

> VIOLA. Of Messaline. Sebastian was my father.
> . . . .
> My father had a mole upon his brow.
> SEBASTIAN. And so had mine.
> VIOLA. And died that day when Viola from her birth
> Had numbered thirteen years.
> SEBASTIAN. Oh, that record is lively in my soul.
> He finished indeed his mortal act
> That day that made my sister thirteen years.

It is as if the pieces are being painstakingly glued together in order to reconstitute the cracked vessel. Once the job is complete, it will be as if nothing had ever been broken.[20]

Sebastian is hardly alone in his cluelessness. Both Orsino and Olivia in *Twelfth Night* have fallen in love with people whose identity—whose class and sex—they entirely mistake. Sebastian's attempt to clarify the situation to his bride would perplex all but the most gifted riddle solvers:

> So comes it, lady, you have been mistook.
> But Nature to her bias drew in that.
> You would have been contracted to a maid.
> Nor are you therein, by my life, deceived:
> You are betrothed both to a maid and man.

When they learn the truth—Cesario is not Orsino's beloved male servant but a girl; Olivia has married not Cesario but Viola's twin brother—they all make the adjustment to the revelations with a speed that belies the possibility of sober reflection:

> since you called me master for so long,
> Here is my hand. You shall from this time be
> Your master's mistress.

Happiness depends less on sorting everything out than on accepting muddle and embracing its consequences.[21]

The end of *Twelfth Night* is in keeping with the reigning confusion that sets the characters lurching from one mistake to another. Similarly, active searching in *The Comedy of Errors* almost immediately gives way to constraint, confusion, and chance. The twins—along with their father and mother—blunder as if in a fog toward the happy ending that they could never have achieved through their conscious efforts. So too the lovers in *A Midsummer Night's Dream* set out into the Athenian woods with a plan that they have talked over, but they quickly succumb to forces over which they have neither control nor understanding. At the end all four have forgotten that they were caught in a web of rivalry, mutual loathing, and betrayal. And it is this forgetting, along with the arbitrary decision of Duke Theseus, that leads to their happiness.

If any of these characters were to ponder deeply what is going on, the happy resolution, the mirth that comes "When earthly things, made even, / Atone together," would be at risk.[22] But what is the right way to achieve this resolution? We get a small glimpse of the answer in the last lines of *The Comedy of Errors* when the twin slaves, Dromio of Syracuse and Dromio of Ephesus, have a moment alone together onstage before proceeding to the celebration. Constantly ordered about, abused, and beaten throughout the play, the two Dromios, sold by their impoverished parents into slavery, could easily complain about their lot and resist the happy mood. Instead one sees the other as a mirror image, a "glass": "Methinks you are my glass and not my brother," he says, "I see, by you, I am a sweet-faced youth." This moment of self-affirmation in the image of the other is followed by a discussion of which of them is the elder and should take precedence in going to the feast. At first they think they should draw straws to determine their order, and then they come up with a better idea, an idea that serves as the last words of the play: "We came into the world like brother and brother, / And now let's go hand in hand, not one before another."[23]

Two qualities in the Dromio twins are striking here: a complete absence of resentment or grudge bearing, either for the immediate abuse that they have suffered or for the lifelong inequity of their condition, and a generous willingness on both their parts to let go any sibling rivalry. That willingness seems enabled by a certain mirrored narcissism: I see that I am handsome by perceiving you as my mirror image.

To this self-congratulatory cheerfulness we can add, as a general principle for achieving happiness, the resilient spirit

shown by *Twelfth Night*'s heroine, Viola. Separated in a shipwreck from her beloved brother, disguised as a man, and desperately in love with her master Orsino, Viola has every reason
to abandon all hope in first chances, both in family and in love.
But she is unaccountably hopeful. She knows that the likeliest
thing is that her brother has drowned, for, as the sea captain
says, it is only "perchance"—that is, by chance—that she is alive.
"Oh, my poor brother!" she laments, and then immediately continues, "And so perchance may he be." "Perchance" as a principle of hope is what keeps Viola buoyant even when the plot
becomes more and more tangled. How can the parts possibly
fit together—"How will this fadge?"—she asks herself, listing
the cross-purposes and mistakes that have led Orsino to love
Olivia, Olivia to love Viola (in her disguise as a man), and Viola
to love Orsino:

> O time, thou must untangle this, not I.
> It is too hard a knot for me t' untie.

She cannot know for certain, of course, that the knot will be
untangled at all, let alone that it will be untangled in a way that
conduces to her happiness, but she is able somehow to main-
tain a basic trust. She is rewarded for this trust by eventually
recovering both her family—in the person of her beloved
brother—and the man for whom she has pined and "sat like
Patience on a monument, / Smiling at grief."[24]

Viola's reward, we might say, is less than perfect. Her
husband-to-be, Orsino, is in the grip of an obsessive and un-
resolved longing for Olivia, a woman who, rejecting him, has
fallen in love with his young servant Cesario—in reality, Viola
in disguise—with whom he has shared his most intimate feelings. He now realizes that this young man is in fact a woman,
and he precipitously declares his intention of marrying her, just

as Olivia has precipitously married the woman's twin brother. In the comedy's famously mad conclusion, Orsino proposes "A solemn combination . . . Of our dear souls." Still calling Viola Cesario—as he will continue to do, he says, until she changes into women's clothes—he will in effect be marrying the man whom the woman he desires has also desired and married. The prospects for Viola's happiness in this peculiar arrangement are unclear, but she has already disclosed what is in effect her key to holding on to the first chance: "O time, thou must untangle this, not I. / It is too hard a knot for me t' untie."[25]

Shakespeare's characters have to confront the fact that their first chance, whether in family or in love, is not securely in their grasp. It can be torn away by accident, stolen by design, menaced by the arbitrary dictates of authority, or buried in confusion. The question they face is what to do in the event of loss and, for that matter, what to do if, in the wake of painful or disillusioning experiences, they recover their first chance. There is no magical formula for those who search for, recover, or successfully cling to a first chance. But the comedies depict a particular range of personal qualities and responses.

At the outer edge is simple obliviousness. Antipholus of Ephesus was too young when the shipwreck split his family asunder to remember anything about the loss. He can look into his birth father's face and claim with perfect confidence, "I never saw my father in my life." So too Guiderius and Arviragus, kidnapped as infants, have no idea of their actual origins and call their kidnapper father. They are all in for a surprise.[26]

Less completely in the dark are those who have hazy impressions of the life they once led. Such in *The Tempest* is Miranda's vague recollection of having many servants attending her when she was a small child, a recollection, she says, that is "far off / And rather like a dream than an assurance." Her father,

Prospero, astonished that she has recalled even this much, goes on to inform her at length of who she was and the world she inhabited before their exile.[27] Similarly, in *The Comedy of Errors* the father has recounted the story of the shipwreck to his son, leading him to set sail to find his missing mother and brother.

Antipholus of Ephesus's search for the missing members of his birth family, seconded by his father's search for him, is paralleled by Prospero's decision after twelve years on his remote island of exile to seize the opportunity that fortune has provided to enable him to restore himself—and his daughter—to the life they had lost. Such direct engagement is characteristic as well of those who attempt to hold on to or regain their first chance in love: the four young lovers in *A Midsummer Night's Dream* rush off to the forest to escape the harsh edict and pursue the object of their desire.

But active striving is not the only or even the most frequent response to the loss of the first chance. After all, Prospero waited twelve years before taking action, which was triggered by the fortuitous proximity of his enemies, and Antipholus had all but given up his search when the play begins. The mothers in both *The Comedy of Errors* and *Pericles* enter convents and evidently harbor no expectation of recovering the families they have lost. Instead of searching, they choose to withdraw from the world, to inhabit a realm that eschews family bonds altogether. At least this is a choice: in *Pericles* the king falls into a clinical depression caused by the "loss / Of a beloved daughter and a wife."[28]

Pericles has given up hope. He is a man "who for this three months hath not spoken / To anyone, nor taken sustenance / But to prorogue his grief." His fortunes are about to change, however: chance brings him together with both his daughter and his wife. Again and again in these plays, it is luck, not striving or calculation, that functions to restore the characters to their first chances. After seven years of futile searching, Antipholus of Syracuse happens to wind up in Ephesus, where his twin, his father, and his mother have all happened to wind up as well. The lovers in *A Midsummer Night's Dream,* unbeknownst to themselves, wandering in confusion in the woods, catch the attention of the fairies, who solve their dilemmas (though not before complicating them further). Expelled from Duke Frederick's court, Rosalind in *As You Like It* takes refuge in the Forest of Arden, where by chance both her lover, Orlando, and her father, the exiled Duke Senior, have also taken refuge. Duke Frederick has raised an army to destroy Duke Senior, but an unforeseen encounter with "an old religious man" converts him, and Duke Senior is restored to his rightful place. The lesson, if there is one to be drawn from any of this, is that much of life is unpredictable and out of one's control.[29]

In a world governed by fortune, active striving may lead only to confusion, and withdrawal to depression. The response that the comedies most prize in their characters, above all in the young heroines, is the resilience that we have noted in Viola and that is shared by Rosalind and Celia in *As You Like It* and by Marina in *Pericles.* There is in these heroines an acceptance of the way things are, even if the way things are is deeply perplexing or uncomfortable or disappointing. But their acceptance is not to be confused with passivity. These characters are all marked by an irrepressible energy that gets them through difficult circumstances and ultimately enables them to recover or to hold on to the first chance in family or in love. This resilience does not seem to be a quality one can acquire; it too is a piece of luck, a personality trait, an endowment not chosen but given.

Perhaps the most striking thing about Shakespeare's vision of the first chance—the object of longing in these plays,

whether as the all-important birth family or as the love that
sweeps away all other considerations—is that it does not demand or bear much thinking about. The characters may crave
it, they may strive to recover or to hold on to it, but they do not
reflect on it or try to understand it. Perhaps Shakespeare thought
that a certain buoyant heedlessness was a condition of the first
chance, or at least of the ability to remain within it.

Going no farther—the refusal or inability to dig more
deeply—extends from the characters to the audience. No one
is encouraged to push too hard on the nature of these relationships. Like the lovers themselves, we are urged to regard what
we have witnessed as a dream: "If we shadows have offended,"
Puck says in the play's epilogue,

> Think but this, and all is mended:
> That you have but slumbered here
> While these visions did appear.
> And this weak and idle theme,
> No more yielding but a dream.

It would be out of order and would threaten the celebration of
the first chance to demand a full reckoning. Better to stay in
the illusion.[30]

2

No Second Chances

Life without the possibility of a second chance is a form of psychological and social confinement that human beings instinctively dread. How does anyone fall into or even elect such an existence, a state Macbeth calls "the sere, the yellow leaf"? Shakespeare was fascinated by all the ways it can happen, whether by choice or accident, treachery or folly.[1]

Early in *Macbeth*, his ambition aroused by his strange encounter with the Weird Sisters on the heath, Macbeth imagines assassinating King Duncan and seizing the crown for himself. Though the opportunity to do so soon arrives, when the king visits his castle as a guest, the would-be assassin decides not to act on his fantasy, which has at once excited and horrified him, but to hold back. After all, he is the king's host, as well as his subject and kinsman. In a famous soliloquy—"If it were done when 'tis done, then 'twere well / It were done quickly"— Macbeth broods about the inevitability with which betrayals like the one he is contemplating "return / To plague the inventor." There can be no way, he recognizes, to escape the consequences of so heinous a deed. "We will proceed no further in this business," he tells his wife.[2]

Why Macbeth proceeds to kill the king, having pains-takingly enumerated the many reasons it would be a disas-trous mistake to do so, is difficult to say. His fatal choice, if it can even be called a choice, is clearly linked to the seductive urging, or rather the sexual pressure, of his wife. "Art thou afeard," Lady Macbeth asks him, "To be the same in thine own act and valor / As thou art in desire?" Macbeth's response to this provocation expresses impatience rather than wavering. "Prithee, peace!" he tells her sharply; "I dare do all that may become a man: / Who dares do more is none." But she renews her challenge—"When you durst do it, then you were a man"— conjoining it with a bizarre claim:

> I have given suck and know
> How tender 'tis to love the babe that milks me;
> I would, while it was smiling in my face,
> Have plucked my nipple from his boneless gums
> And dashed the brains out, had I so sworn as you
> Have done to this.

It is these words that unfix Macbeth's resolution to remain loyal to the king. "If we should fail?" he asks nervously, expressing doubts that his wife knows perfectly how to allay. After a few more exchanges, he is determined to proceed: "I am settled, and bend up / Each corporal agent to this terrible feat."[3]

What is it about Lady Macbeth's image of dashing her infant's brains out that leads Macbeth to make the decision to go ahead with the assassination? If anything, the imagined vi-olation of one of humanity's deepest moral and psychological inhibitions makes the pair's underlying motivation seem more opaque, not less. As a form of psychological warfare, sexual teasing—"When you durst do it, then you were a man"—makes some sense. But the image of infanticide should only confirm

Macbeth's queasy awareness that the betrayal he is contemplating is the most extreme imaginable ethical transgression, and it therefore sharpens the question of why he would choose to proceed.

The play refuses to answer the question. Macbeth is being drawn toward an act "Whose horrid image doth unfix my hair / And make my seated heart knock at my ribs." He who had earlier been praised for unseaming one of the king's enemies "from the nave to the chops" grasps that in killing the king he will be unseaming himself. Even when he first entertained as fantasy the idea of the assassination, the mere image of the act in his mind made him feel that he was falling apart:

> My thought, whose murder yet is but fantastical,
> Shakes so my single state of man
> That function is smothered in surmise,
> And nothing is but what is not.

Recognizing that it would be self-destructive to carry out the plot, he has had second thoughts and called it off.[4]

But something in his wife and perhaps in Macbeth himself is at war with these second thoughts. He seems to be driven to resist his own recovery and to close off the possibility of a second chance. Lady Macbeth's infanticidal fantasy manages to convey to her husband a sense of absolute, unshakable obligation—"had I so sworn as you / Have done"—that confers something like inevitability on what a moment before had seemed anything but inevitable.

That air of inevitability in turn reaches back to the very early moments of the play, when the Weird Sisters hail Macbeth as he "that shalt be king hereafter!" Yet their prophetic words only make the issue of Macbeth's choice more difficult to answer. "I'll do, I'll do, and I'll do," one of the Weird Sisters chants, but what it is that all of them do remains tantalizingly unclear, as does the scope of Macbeth's actual freedom to choose. For a moment, at least, Macbeth speaks as if he possessed such freedom—"We will proceed no further in this business"—but a moment later he is convinced, or he convinces himself, that he has no power to reverse his course. And when that night he takes the fatal steps toward the king's bedchamber, he is convinced, or he convinces himself, that a spectral dagger—whether a "fatal vision" or "a dagger of the mind" he cannot tell—is marshaling him the way he is going.[5]

Could Macbeth still have turned around at this point—with King Duncan sleeping peacefully—and returned to his wife and to a different outcome, a lifetime of other choices and other chances? Why doesn't he follow his wise intention, manifestly in his own best interest, to remain loyal and bask in the honors that the king had showered upon him? Why does someone, fully conscious that what he is about to do is self-destructive, go ahead and do it anyway? These are the kinds of questions that Freud pondered throughout his career, concluding that the answers must lie deep within the psyche of the person in the grip of a compulsion. Shakespeare evidently shared this conclusion—the soliloquies provide access to Macbeth's psyche—and yet the play goes out of its way to make it impossible to reach any clear answers about why he destroys his own happiness. The words Macbeth speaks to himself as he nears the moment of his terrible act seem deliberately to collapse the interval and close off any alternative. It is as if, as a defense against further anguished second thoughts, he is actively driving himself forward: "I go, and it is done."[6]

After it is done—after the king lies murdered in his bed, "his silver skin laced with his golden blood"—Macbeth has irrevocably entered a life without the possibility of a second chance. His nightmarish existence consists of committing crime after crime, and he cannot stop. "I am in blood / Stepped so far," he confides to his wife, "that, should I wade no more, / Returning were as tedious as to go o'er." Equally "tedious," as he puts it, precisely because it makes no difference, except of course to those whose lives he will destroy; for Macbeth and his wife, in any case, it is all the same.[7]

Shortly before he is killed, Macbeth describes what it feels like to live without the possibility of a second chance—that is, without freedom and without hope. Such a life is a succession of days—"tomorrow and tomorrow and tomorrow"—indistinguishable from one another, however much each may be filled with events. Time, drained of any meaning, is a form of emptiness. "It is a tale / Told by an idiot, full of sound and fury, / Signifying nothing."[8]

As there is early in *Macbeth,* so there is in almost all of Shakespeare's tragedies a moment in which the hero is offered the glimpse of an escape route, a way to avert his fate and seize instead upon a different outcome. The moment of crisis is often signaled by a warning or omen. Near the beginning of *Julius Caesar,* a soothsayer cries out in a shrill voice, telling Caesar to beware the Ides of March, but Caesar dismisses him as "a dreamer." Then the Ides of March comes round with an almost absurd succession of cautionary signals. During the preceding night there are violent storms. In her sleep Calpurnia cries out, "Help, ho! They murder Caesar!" The morning brings reports of weird apparitions: a lioness whelping in the street, graves opening and yielding up their dead, blood dripping on the Capitol, and so on. The augurs, reading the entrails of sacrificial animals, urge Caesar not to stir from his house. All the bad omens, together with the urgent pleas of his wife, lead Caesar to decide that he will change his plans and not go, as he had intended, to the Senate House. "I will stay at home," he declares.[9]

Appealing to his vanity and ambition, the cunning words

of one of the conspirators induce Caesar to set out after all toward his fatal appointment, but even then the result is not settled. A man named Artemidorus has somehow gotten wind of the conspiracy and has laid out the details—complete with names—in a letter. He hopes to hand the letter to the intended victim as he passes along the street on his way to the Senate House: "If thou read this, O Caesar, thou mayst live." But when Artemidorus tries desperately to press the letter into Caesar's hands, his very urgency backfires:

> ARTEMIDORUS. O Caesar, read mine first, for mine's a
> suit
>   That touches Caesar nearer. Read it, great
>   Caesar.
> CAESAR. What touches us ourself shall be last served.
> ARTEMIDORUS. Delay not, Caesar, read it instantly.
> CAESAR. What, is the fellow mad?

Nothing more is made of this moment. We never learn anything further about Artemidorus—he simply disappears from the play—or how he found out what was being planned. His warning, however, reminds us that the course of world history could have been different.[10]

Once they have occurred, events take on an air of inevitability, but if we reenter them imaginatively, as Shakespeare's play invites us to do, we can recover a sense of contingency. None of the key actors at the time knew how the situation would work out; each of them could have swerved left rather than right, decided to stay home, had a change of heart. Had he read Artemidorus's letter—or listened to his wife, or attended to the omens, or taken the soothsayer seriously—Caesar might have escaped the knives that were awaiting him in the Senate House. Shocked by the murderous anger he had aroused even among those he regarded as his friends, he could have tempered his ambition, just as Brutus could have reconsidered his course of action, and the two of them, along with the Roman Republic, would have had a longer lease on life. All those whose fates were sealed on March 15, 44 BCE, might have had a second chance.

Or perhaps we are meant to conclude exactly the opposite. Perhaps the flurry of failed warnings and ignored omens suggests that there are no second chances, however much their possibility may hover before us. Perhaps everything has all been determined beforehand, with the same unalterable fixity that it seems to have when we look backward through the lens of history. After all, Caesar's assassination is one of those events that has the hard certainty of a rock. Counterfactuals do not count. And its explanation, Shakespeare's play suggests, may be found not in metaphysical mysteries hidden in entrails but in far more mundane causes. Caesar's personality—his vanity and overconfidence—would always have kept him from attending to any warning, the concentration of power in a charismatic general had already fatally undermined the republic, and Rome was destined to descend into civil war. Artemidorus's warning exists in the play only to show that it was and had to be ignored. It is like the message in Kafka's parable that the Chinese emperor on his deathbed whispers into the ear of a messenger to deliver to you and you alone: no matter how powerful the imperial messenger, he will not manage to get through the crowds in the vast palace and the still vaster city, let alone to reach you in your remote corner of the empire. You can only daydream of the message that you will never in fact receive.

At the opening of *King Lear*, as at the opening of *Julius Caesar*, the state is teetering at the brink of disaster. The aged Lear, having declared his intention to divide his kingdom among his three daughters, stages a love test to determine the final distribution of land. When Cordelia, his youngest daughter, fails to flatter him, he curses her and proposes to divide her share between his two older daughters. His faithful servant Kent, trying to ward off the catastrophe he sees all too clearly is happening, puts his warning in terms that rival Artemidorus's plainness, and in this case the message does reach the ears of its intended recipient:

> Reserve thy state,
> And in thy best consideration check
> This hideous rashness. Answer my life my judgement,
> Thy youngest daughter does not love thee least,
> Nor are those empty-hearted whose low sounds
> Reverb no hollowness.

But this warning too is to no avail: Lear casts out his one true daughter and entrusts himself and his realm to the false ones.[11]

Cordelia's measured response to the love test—"I love your majesty / According to my bond, no more nor less"—has disappointed and angered Lear. He feels bitterly disillusioned: "I loved her most, and thought to rest my rest / On her kind nursery." What he would need to escape this disillusionment—to fashion in its wake a more viable relationship with his daughter—is to become disillusioned with himself. But there is something in his character, as there is in Caesar's, that keeps him from entertaining the possibility that he is mistaken and hence from obtaining the possibility of a second chance. Lear's whole life has filled him with fantasies of omnipotence. To question his own judgment—and thereby revoke the curse he has uttered upon his youngest daughter—he would have to open a space, as he puts it, "betwixt our sentence and our power." And everything both in his personality and in the structure of the absolutist world he inhabits and by which he has been formed is designed to keep that space from opening.[12]

The principal victim of Lear's intransigent folly is obviously Cordelia, but Goneril and Regan must be counted as its victims as well. All three are injured by the contest he has staged: "Which of you shall we say doth love us most?" The older sisters comply in extravagant terms. "I love you more than words can wield the matter," Goneril begins; "Dearer than eyesight, space, and liberty; / Beyond what can be valued, rich or rare, / No less than life." Regan's declaration is if anything still more extreme:

> I profess
> Myself an enemy to all other joys
> Which the most precious square of sense possesses,
> And find I am alone felicitate
> In your dear highness' love.

There is, she claims, no happiness in her life apart from the love of her father.[13]

In her refusal to join in this contest and give Lear what he wants, Cordelia brings out the vaguely incestuous implication of the odd phrase, "the most precious square of sense." She makes clear that her father's demand, if taken seriously, would leave no room for her or her sisters to fashion their own lives:

> Why have my sisters husbands if they say
> They love you all? Haply when I shall wed
> That lord whose hand must take my plight shall carry
> Half my love with him, half my care and duty.
> Sure, I shall never marry like my sisters
> To love my father all.

By failing to set any boundaries to the love he craves from his children, indeed by demanding from them displays of limitless ardor, Lear is threatening their future prospects for love, love that is always fashioned, as Cordelia perceives, out of a portion of childhood feelings that are transferred—"carried," as she puts it—to a new object of desire. If that transfer is blocked—if she is forbidden to carry some part of the child's love she has felt for her father over to the relationship she will forge with her spouse—then there can be for her or her sisters no adult love. Don't you understand, she is in effect asking her father, don't you understand that the love that lies on the other side of childhood is always a second chance? She shall never, she emphatically declares, love her father "all"—"all" is the issue, since absolute, limitless love for the parent would preclude love for anyone else. If she is to love and be loved as an adult, half her care and duty will belong to someone else. If this means that her father will have to accept a diminished share of her love, so be it. Such is the fate of parents if children are to leave home and have lives of their own.[14]

Lear is virtually ensuring that his daughters will be hypocrites. Having decided, as he puts it, "to shake all cares and business from our age," he is transferring all his land to his daughters, who will in return become his guardians. But in demanding from them expressions of absolute love, he has forgotten his role as the guardian of their ability to become adults, to form relationships, to find love. He stages the love test in the presence of the husbands of his two eldest daughters and with the two suitors for his youngest daughter's hand waiting in the wings. By treating love as a high-stakes competitive game and demanding that they formally wager all of it for him, he is forcing them to lie.[15]

As adults Goneril and Regan live in an awareness of the chasm between their professions—what they have had to say in order to gain their ends—and their true feelings. Only Cor-

delia escapes this trap by refusing to play the game, though she
pays a high price for doing so in bearing the brunt of her father's disappointment and rage. Still, she alone of the three
daughters retains the possibility of loving her father, as she puts
it, according to her bond. Her older sisters only wish him dead.
And as if forever locked in the nightmare of their father's game,
Goneril and Regan end their lives in a kind of love test, a murderous sexual competition for the cynical Edmund, who is
coolly indifferent to them both.

   When the reality of Lear's new situation settles in, after
he has disinherited Cordelia and divided his kingdom between
his two vicious daughters, Lear begins to have second thoughts:
"I did her wrong." But by then it is too late. In tragedy, second
chances are invariably refused when they are still possible and
longed for when they are not. *King Lear* depicts this longing
both in the ruined king's increasingly intense regret for what
he has done to his youngest daughter and in his wild but im-
potent threats against the others: "I will do such things— / What
they are, yet I know not, but they shall be / The terrors of the
earth!" It is all for nothing; the damage has been done, and he
cannot undo it.[16]

   Goneril and Regan urge their now powerless father to accept this new phase of his life. "You are old," Regan tells him,

> You should be ruled and led
> By some discretion that discerns your state
> Better than you yourself.

But senescence—what Jaques in *As You Like It* calls "second
childishness and mere oblivion / Sans eyes, sans teeth, sans taste,
sans everything"—is hardly the second chance Lear craves and
for which he may at last be psychologically ready. For he is fi-

nally experiencing the awakening that, had he been capable of it earlier, might have saved him: "They told me I was everything: 'tis a lie."[17]

Things fall apart: Lear's older daughters strip him of his authority, his attendants, and his dignity; he wanders about shouting to the heavens in a howling storm; he descends into madness; he collapses in utter physical and mental exhaustion. And then the old, ruined man awakens to see standing before him his youngest daughter, who has returned from France with an army in an attempt to save him. Against all odds, their reunion seems ripe with the possibility of a second chance.

Disoriented and confused, Lear speaks out of a profound and necessary self-disillusionment:

> I am a very foolish, fond old man,
> Fourscore and upward,
> Not an hour more nor less,
> And to deal plainly,
> I fear I am not in my perfect mind.

Then, almost miraculously this disillusionment enables him for the first time to see his daughter, actually to see her as she is, and to acknowledge her existence not as a mere extension of his own ego but, in his tentative words, as a woman:

> Do not laugh at me,
> For, as I am a man, I think this lady
> To be my child Cordelia.

She kneels down to receive the parental blessing he had earlier withheld; he kneels down to beg her forgiveness. After the play's seemingly endless descent into cruelty and horror, we finally glimpse for this suffering pair a path upward and out. But the

path is almost immediately blocked by forces beyond the control of either Lear or Cordelia. A war is being waged, and in the
decisive battle both king and daughter are captured. What had
seemed almost within reach vanishes.[18]

The larger point, made repeatedly in Shakespeare's tragedies, is that access to a second chance is not solely a function
of emotional readiness or an effort of will. Circumstances—
here freedom, but it could also be financial resources, social
structures, institutional mechanisms, or a host of other constraints—have to be in place. Over most of these circumstances
individuals have little or no agency. There is in tragic outcomes,
as in happy comic twists of fate, a strong element of chance.
Readiness—emotional readiness—is crucial but it is certainly
not all.

Taken prisoner, Lear consoles himself with what he imagines will be a second chance—a shared intimacy with his beloved daughter, in confinement, to be sure, but somehow all
the better for that reason:

> Come, let's away to prison.
> We two alone will sing like birds i' th' cage.
> When thou dost ask me blessing, I'll kneel down
> And ask of thee forgiveness. So we'll live,
> And pray, and sing, and tell old tales, and laugh
> At gilded butterflies, and hear poor rogues
> Talk of court news, and we'll talk with them too—
> Who loses, and who wins; who's in, who's out—
> And take upon's the mystery of things,
> As if we were God's spies.

For all the poignancy of this fantasy, it signals a failure on Lear's
part to grasp the reality of the situation, and not only because
the victors would never allow the king and his daughter to sur-

vive for any length of time. The brief moment in which he took in the reality of his daughter as an independent being and could register something of her feelings has all but vanished. To his dream of spending long years together singing like birds in a cage, Cordelia says absolutely nothing. This would hardly be her idea of a second chance.[19]

Yet the idea of their second chance still somehow hangs in the air, as if the characters—or the play itself—could not survive without it. Near the end of *King Lear* the king, howling with grief and rage, comes onstage carrying the body of his daughter Cordelia. "She's gone forever," he says flatly, "I know when one is dead and when one lives. / She's dead as earth." Then immediately he belies his bleak certainty by looking for signs that she might after all be alive. To catch the faintest sign that she is still breathing, he holds up to her lips first a mirror and then a feather. "This feather stirs," he cries, "She lives!"[20]

To those in Shakespeare's audience who knew the Lear story from its many retellings, the cry must have seemed at once predictable and gratifying. From Geoffrey of Monmouth's twelfth-century *History of the Kings of Britain* all the way through the version that had been onstage only a few years before Shakespeare's play, Cordelia survives, and, reunited with her father, rules the land. Though old Lear had made a disastrous misjudgment in crediting the false flattery of his older daughters and in disowning his youngest for speaking the truth, after great suffering he and his kingdom manage to see their way through to a happy ending. Restoration and a second chance were the whole point of the story. "If it be so," as Shakespeare's Lear says, when he sees, or thinks he sees, the feather stirring, "It is a chance which does redeem all sorrows / That ever I have felt."[21]

But after dangling before the audience this redemptive possibility, Shakespeare snatches it away. The crazed father veers back and forth between the agonizing truth—"Thou'lt come no more, / Never, never, never, never, never"—and the dream of redemption: "Do you see this? Look on her! Look, her lips, / Look there. Look there!" We are forced to grasp, however, that there is no "chance" that will redeem Lear's sorrows. In the first act Lear in effect put an end to his daughter when she failed to give him the gratification he wanted, and it has taken the remainder of the play to work through the full consequences of his rash words. "She's gone forever."[22]

By the play's close, the didactic lesson that was the apparent motivation of the original story seems to have vanished. We could still say that Lear should have listened to the good Kent's warning, that he should have checked his own rashness and questioned his own judgment, that he should have observed his children more attentively, and so forth and so on, but this is only to wish that Lear had been a different person from the one he was, the one his world had made him. Early in the play one of the wicked daughters remarks about their father that "he hath ever but slenderly known himself." True enough. Yet at the end none of the surviving characters is inclined to make moral judgments upon him. The closest anyone comes is in Edgar's monosyllabic words near the close, words that in effect reflect back on the opening scene of the love test, on the unbearable demands that parents make on children and on the lies that children tell their parents: "Speak what we feel, not what we ought to say."[23]

Shakespeare's most intense exploration of tragedy as the absence of a second chance is *Othello,* whose villain, Iago, first poisons the happiness of the newly wed Othello and Desdemona and then repeatedly plays with the possibility of recovery only to block it. Iago deftly plants the suspicion in Othello's mind that Desdemona is unfaithful. "My life upon her faith," Othello had proclaimed before the Venetian Senate following their elopement, so it makes sense that his secret enemy, determined to destroy that life, would attempt to undermine his faith. This is cruel enough, but the cruelty is immeasurably heightened by the villain's sly playing with Othello's hope that the suspicion is unjust and that his fears are groundless. "I perchance am vicious in my guess," Iago declares, describing with unnerving candor what he is doing,

> As, I confess, it is my nature's plague
> To spy into abuses and of my jealousy
> Shape faults that are not.

Therefore, he slyly urges Othello not to take any notice, "nor build yourself a trouble" out of mere "scattering and unsure observance." Each of these perfectly just observations is poison that, taking the form of reassurance, mimes the counsel a friend might offer to heal a breach of faith: "Oh, beware, my lord, of jealousy! . . . I am to pray you not to strain my speech / To grosser issues. . . . My lord, I would I might entreat your honor / To scan this thing no farther." Iago is the master saboteur of second chances. Occupying the role of friend and twisting his words toward heightening, not allaying, suspicion, he in effect blocks one of the principal avenues that might ordinarily enable someone to find a way out of disillusionment and rebuild a threatened or damaged relationship.[24]

As soon as the poison has begun its work, Iago shifts tactics and attempts to counteract any sign of backsliding from the mistrust he has successfully engendered. When, in the midst of his pain, Othello says of Desdemona, "A fair woman! A sweet woman!," Iago quickly rejoins, "Nay, you must forget that." "Oh, the world hath not a sweeter creature," Othello continues; "she might lie by an emperor's side, and command him tasks," to which Iago replies, "Nay, that's not your way."[25]

The villain is hard at work, warding off the possibility in Othello of any recovery from his disillusionment and hence the possibility of a second chance. Desdemona makes Iago's task more difficult by the clarity of her innocence and her uncanny way of allowing Othello's anger the option of turning back into desire. "Be as your fancies teach you," she responds, when he asks her to leave him; "Whate'er you be, I am obedient." As the play makes abundantly clear, this is not the manifestation of meekness; Desdemona is perfectly capable of standing up for herself: "By heaven, you do me wrong!" But even in the midst of her pain and confusion, she is holding on to the love that first united them and that she continues to feel. "I would you had never seen him," says her maid Emilia, to which Desdemona, readying herself for bed, replies,

> So would not I: my love doth so approve him
> That even his stubbornness, his checks, his frowns
> —Prithee, unpin me—have grace and favor.

That little touch as she undresses and readies herself for bed—"Prithee, unpin me"—is a subtle reflection of the longing for the renewal of love to which she clings to the very end.[26]

That the longing survives in Othello too only intensifies his pain: "But yet the pity of it, Iago. O Iago, the pity of it, Iago!" To this lament, so intense that it threatens his plot, Iago responds with a demonic parody of what a second chance would be. "If you are so fond over her iniquity, give her patent to offend; for if it touch not you, it comes near nobody." Why not make peace with the way things have turned out, let her have her lover, and simply continue? Iago perfectly calculates the effect of this humiliating suggestion. Othello explodes with murderous rage: "I will chop her into messes!"[27]

Iago's aim is to drive Othello toward the act from which

there can be no return, no second chances. As, lamp in hand, he approaches his sleeping wife, Othello broods on the consequences of what he is contemplating doing:

> Put out the light, and then put out the light.
> If I quench thee, thou flaming minister,
> I can again thy former light restore,
> Should I repent me—but once put out thy light,
> Thou cunning'st pattern of excelling nature,
> I know not where is that Promethean heat
> That can thy light relume.

"Relume" is Shakespeare's own coinage for the act of rekindling that Othello knows can be done with an extinguished candle but not with an extinguished life. Nonetheless, in the conviction that there is no way to recover their ruptured marriage and in the delusion that he is somehow serving the cause of justice, he smothers her.[28]

Even then Shakespeare is not entirely willing to give up the dream of the second chance; rather he uses that dream to heighten the sense of tragedy. From behind the curtains Othello has drawn around her bed, the dying Desdemona cries out three separate times, the third and final time an expression of her enduring love: "Commend me to my kind lord. Oh, farewell!" It is as if the play insists on driving home, even to the murdered woman's last breath, what cannot be "relumed," what Othello has tragically thrown away.[29]

Christianity in Shakespeare's time, as for centuries before and after, looked to life after death as a kind of last chance. There would be no multiple returns in different forms, as some Eastern religions believed. And there would not be a mere sinking into darkness, as the Jews believed. The afterlife was the place where all scores would be settled and the truth revealed. Those who suffered unjustly in this life would enjoy the bliss that they so richly deserved; those who had managed to evade the punishment that was their due would suffer for all eternity. But without explicitly venturing into forbidden theological territory, Shakespeare's tragedies call this whole apparatus of belief into question.

In Shakespeare's vision the afterlife has not altogether vanished. It is never dismissed, as it is in Freud, as an illusion. His characters can invoke it, long for it, fear it, without arousing skepticism or contempt. For Shakespeare, as for his contemporaries, it is not a symptom but rather a psychological and spiritual resource; "Good night, sweet prince," mourns Horatio over the dead body of Hamlet, "And flights of angels sing thee to thy rest." But none of the famously knotty problems in *Hamlet* is remotely resolved by this pious hope. If anything, Horatio's words call attention to the moral and theological issues that tormented the hero for whom the afterlife was the "undiscovered country from whose bourn / No traveler returns." So too at the end of *Othello*, addressing Desdemona's lifeless body, Othello says, "This look of thine will hurl my soul from heaven, / And fiends will snatch at it." Horrified by what he has done, he welcomes the thought of these torments:

> Whip me, ye devils,
> From the possession of this heavenly sight;
> Blow me about in winds, roast me in sulfur,
> Wash me in steep-down gulfs of liquid fire.

But nothing in *Othello* encourages us to take these fantasies literally or to imagine postmortem rewards or punishments as the resolution of the tragic story we have witnessed. The overwhelming emphasis is on the finality of the putting out of the light. The most the play can offer as resolution is Othello's suicide and the prospect that Iago, who steadfastly refuses to explain why he has done what he has done, will be tortured. For neither of them—any more than for Desdemona or Emilia or Roderigo—will there be a second chance.[30]

3

Second Chances and Delinquency

Shakespeare's most famous juvenile delinquent is a prince. The eldest son of King Henry IV and heir apparent to the English throne, Prince Hal prefers to spend his time not among the ruling elite, where he belongs, but in a tavern, in the company of whores, thieves, drunkards, loud-mouthed ruffians, and an amusing but particularly scoundrelly fat knight. The king, seeing "riot and dishonor stain the brow" of his wayward son, despairs that he will ever amount to anything. "The hope and expectation of thy time / Is ruined," he tells Hal, "and the soul of every man / Prophetically do forethink thy fall."[1]

The king's pessimism is not unreasonable. He looks around, as parents tend to do, and sees that other young men his son's age are far more accomplished and promising. He finds it particularly galling that the son of one of his enemies is already widely renowned for his martial feats and gallantry, while Hal is idling away his time with lowlifes. How could this have happened? At his son's age, the father reflects, he was a paragon of political ambition and strategic calculation. That is how he reached his exalted position. Now his own son is not merely shirking his responsibility as heir but actively undermining everything his father has painstakingly achieved and threatening the country's well-being. By keeping such bad company— people who are vulgar, notorious, unruly, law breaking, and unredeemable—Hal is making a mockery of the authority on which any stable order necessarily depends.

Hal's actual tavern life, as Shakespeare depicts it in *1 Henry IV,* is full of laughter, centered above all in the larger-than-life figure of Falstaff. True, Falstaff is gluttonous, mendacious, and disreputable, but his wit, his enormous appetite for pleasure, and his relentless skewering of the lies and illusions that govern society make him an irresistible alternative symbolic father to the sour and anxious Henry IV. Given a choice, why should Hal *not* opt for Carnival over Lent? Carnival is what Hal's way of life—his "vile participation," as the king contemptuously puts it—feels like from the inside.[2]

It might seem, then, that delinquency is Hal's version of a second chance. Repudiating the status into which he was born, he has chosen a new identity, transforming himself into the carefree boon companion Falstaff calls his "sweet wag." But Hal regards the life he is living not as an achieved identity but rather as a way station toward the genuine second chance that he intends to fashion at some as yet undetermined point in the future. As long as that second chance hovers ahead of him as a kind of promissory note he intends one day to redeem, it is as if he carries a secret license to transgress. He can tell himself that he is free to indulge in whatever behavior appeals to him without incurring any permanent stain. He can amuse himself in the company of whores and thugs, join Falstaff in mocking his father, even participate in an armed robbery of the king's own revenue officers. He can act up and act out, pretending to be someone he is not, and marvel at his own boldness: "Well then, once in my days I'll be a madcap." Though he was born into the very topmost rank of a strictly hierarchical society, the company he keeps enables him to learn something of a lower world he was never meant to enter, and he is a quick study. "They call drinking deep 'dyeing scarlet,'" he reports of his boozing mates, "and when you breathe in your watering they cry 'Hem!' and bid you 'Play it off!' To conclude, I am so good a proficient in one quarter of an hour that I can drink with any tinker in his language during my life."[3]

But the tavern is not his world, and he knows it. For that matter, so do his companions: they do not imagine for a moment that Hal is one of them or that the life he is currently leading is his true second chance. They too grasp that it is an interval, a charmed pause, before he assumes the role that he is destined to play in life—in their lives and in his own. ("I prithee, sweet wag," Falstaff asks him, "shall there be gallows standing in England when thou art king?") What his companions do not grasp—although Falstaff may have an uneasy intimation of it— is that this interval is a piece of cold calculation very much like those on which his royal father prided himself.[4]

Hal reveals this calculation early in the play. Alone after his tavern mates have left the room, he allows himself one of his very few moments of intimate self-revelation. "I know you all," he says about those with whom he has just been merrily planning a new escapade. He may appear to treat them as his good friends, but in reality he regards them as "base contagious clouds" that smother up the sun, until that sun, "breaking through the foul and ugly mists / Of vapours that did seem to strangle him," reveals its beauty to a wondering world. In his imagination, then, Hal is a sun—and a son—who is deliberately hiding himself. His second chance will come when he emerges from the darkness and blazes all the more brilliantly for having been withheld from view.[5]

Hal views his delinquency as strategic, and its effect seems to confirm this view. After all, it makes his father—preoccupied as he is with his own survival in a ruthless game of thrones—pay attention to him, worry about him, miss him, call for him. Even the bitter rebukes, sharp as they are, signal a parental concern that the cold-blooded Henry might not otherwise manifest. At the same time the tavern gives the crown prince—who is, by virtue of his position, what Ophelia in *Hamlet* calls "the observed of all observers"—some small measure of privacy, some space to play and experiment.[6] To experiment at what? At becoming his own person, and not the exact replica his father wishes him to be. That replica—Henry the son of Henry—is in effect Hal's first chance, the role he was born to play, and it is one from which he wishes to escape as if his life depended on it. Indeed his life—the life he hopes to live and perhaps his very survival—may actually depend on this escape. Shakespeare goes out of his way to show in Hal's rival Hotspur the fatal consequence of being the dream son. Hal knows that he will, if he lives long enough, succeed to the throne, but he is determined to make that inherited identity feel like a second chance. Deviating from the straight path is his way forward.

Shakespeare found this strategic fashioning of a second chance through delinquency fascinating enough to make it the subject of two plays, *1* and *2 Henry IV*. In both, he emphasized the risks of the strategy, as well as its rewards. There is at least a chance that the lure of the delinquency, its transgressive pleasures, will be strong enough to keep hold of the delinquent indefinitely. "The true prince," as Falstaff puts it, "may, for recreation sake, prove a false thief."[7] Notwithstanding his secret vision of the future—the promissory note that he clings to in his mind—Hal may never emerge from behind the clouds. In the meantime, he has alienated the whole governing class. The king's counselors dismiss him as worthless, and the king's rebellious enemies treat him as a laughingstock. His younger brothers fear him and keep their distance. His father, responding to the aggression and rejection implicit in his behavior, regards Hal more as a mortal enemy, one who wishes his death, than as a loving son.

Hal's friend and surrogate father, Falstaff, is richly amusing, but his irresponsibility is clearly dangerous. During a rebellion against the regime, he pockets the conscription money he has been given to form a strong military regiment for the decisive battle and collects instead a cut-rate assembly of living scarecrows. When Hal says he never saw such pitiful rascals, Falstaff's reply makes clear his utter contempt for the whole enterprise: "Tut, tut, good enough to toss; food for powder, food for powder. They'll fill a pit as well as better." This cynicism may be bracing and well deserved, but if the rebels defeat the king's forces, the king will be killed, and there will be no question of a second chance for Hal, for he too will certainly be killed.[8]

Nonetheless, Falstaff remains the gravitational center of Hal's truancy. In his orbit the prince has the opportunity to escape the heavy responsibilities attendant on his birth, the social constraints of his class, the oppressive expectations of his father and his father's allies. "You follow the young Prince up and down like his ill angel," the Lord Chief Justice complains to Falstaff, but Falstaff replies, with considerable justification, that it is the prince who is following him around: "I cannot rid my hands of him."[9]

Small wonder. His father's court, preoccupied with conspiracy, disorder, and rebellion, has scarcely room for a smile, let alone a laugh. Falstaff, by contrast, is a comic genius. "The brain of this foolish-compounded clay, man," he observes about himself, "is not able to invent anything that tends to laughter more than I invent, or is invented on me." The last phrase is telling. Falstaff knows that a major part of his charm is the laughter he provokes among those who think they are making fun of him, and, far from defending himself against this laughter, in order to be the only stand-up comedian in the room he lends himself to it and encourages it. "I am not only witty in myself," he says, "but the cause that wit is in other men." In Falstaff's company, Hal, the son of a relentless, sober father, discovers that he himself is (or thinks he is—it amounts to almost the same thing) wonderfully witty.[10]

Falstaff's charm does not work on everyone. He tries it out on Hal's younger brother, Prince John, without any success at all. "This same young sober-blooded boy doth not love me," he admits, "nor a man cannot make him laugh." In order for comedy to work, there must be an inclination to welcome it, and Prince John utterly lacks the inclination: "But that's no marvel," Falstaff observes, "he drinks no wine."[11]

The comedian knows that laughs are harder to come by without what Shakespeare's age called "belly cheer." And as the presiding genius—or so he hopes—of his protégé's second chance, Falstaff also knows that it is in drink that people often experience a transformation of the self. He spins an elaborate quasi-medical theory of how wine (his preference is for the white fortified Spanish wine known as sherry sack) brings about this transformation, by drying up "all the foolish and dull and cruddy vapors" in the brain and making it "full of nimble, fiery, and delectable shapes." Hal might have wound up like his stiff, humorless younger brother, but, under Falstaff's expert tutelage, "the cold blood he did naturally inherit of his father he hath, like lean, sterile, and bare land, manured, husbanded, and tilled, with excellent endeavor of drinking good and good store of fertile sherry."[12]

This picture of Hal's cold-blooded father—lean, sterile, bare—goes a long way toward explaining why for the son the sleazy warmth of the tavern, the collective pranks and laughter, and Falstaff's bulging, sweaty, profligate presence hold such intense allure. Falstaff has a further allure, which lies in what we might call the candor of his dishonesty. He constantly lies and cheats, he refuses to pay his debts, and he takes advantage of anyone foolish enough to trust him. At least among his friends, he makes no secret of these predatory qualities, and when he occasionally speaks in the accents of wronged innocence or puritanical sobriety, everyone in his inner circle is in on the joke. For Hal this open fraudulence is in stark contrast to what he perceives as his father's hidden hypocrisy, hypocrisy so deeply ingrained, so structurally necessary to the survival of the entire regime, that it leaves no room anywhere in his vicinity for candid acknowledgment, let alone laughter.

In a past about which no one can safely speak, Henry, as his son is well aware, had led a successful rebellion, connived at the murder of the anointed king he had overthrown, and then assumed for himself the trappings of royal legitimacy. At the end of an earlier history play, *Richard II*, Shakespeare had perfectly captured the moral incoherence of the usurper's position. When the murderer, who has acted upon Henry's instigation, comes for his reward, Henry sends him instead into exile: "Though I did wish him dead," he acknowledges, "I hate the murderer, love him murdered." Having refused to give any payment for carrying out his will, the king then proposes to make a voyage to the Holy Land, "To wash this blood off from my guilty hand."[13]

Nothing in the *Henry IV* plays suggests a resolution to this fundamental, defining contradiction. On the contrary, part 1 begins when Henry's proposed expiatory voyage to the Holy Land is brought to a sudden halt by a dangerous rebellion at home led by his former allies, while in part 2, having finally crushed that rebellion through a blend of military force and duplicity, the king dies in a chamber that ironically is called Jerusalem. So much for washing the blood off from his guilty hands.

As he lies dying, Henry confesses to his son "By what bypaths and indirect crooked ways / I met this crown," but Hal already knows all about those crooked ways and has grown up in the poisoned atmosphere bred by them.[14]

Hal's is a paradigmatic case of what at a certain point befalls almost all perceptive children: the painful recognition of the lies and hypocrisy that govern parental and social authority. Rebellion in Hal's case takes the form of a surrogate father who is no hypocrite because he is so open in his fraudulence. One of Falstaff's recurrent comic routines—he never quite tires of it—is to speak in the accents of fallen virtue: "Thou hast done much harm upon me, Hal; God forgive thee for it. Before I knew thee, Hal, I knew nothing, and now am I, if a man should speak truly, little better than one of the wicked. I must give over this life, and I will give it over." And then a moment later, when he is teased for having just agreed to participate in a robbery, "Why, Hal, 'tis my vocation, Hal. 'Tis no sin for a man to labor in his vocation." For Hal, the particular piquancy of this comedy is the implicit parody of his father's hypocritical moralism, a parody made explicit when Falstaff directly impersonates the king pompously reproaching his son:

> There is a thing, Harry, which thou hast often heard
> of, and it is known to many in our land by the name
> of pitch. This pitch, as ancient writers do report, doth
> defile; so doth the company thou keepest. For, Harry,
> now I do not speak to thee in drink but in tears; not
> in pleasure but in passion; not in words only but in
> woes also.

Hal does not have to accuse his father of speaking in bad faith; Falstaff does it for him with delicious irreverence.[15]

But for the delinquent prince this exercise in disillusionment—this imaginary second chance based on exposing the father as the hypocrite he is—is only momentary, indirect, and provisional. At the end of this memorable scene Hal switches roles and, now impersonating his father, condemns "that trunk of humors, that bolting-hutch of beastliness, that swollen parcel of dropsies, that huge bombard of sack, that stuffed cloak-bag of guts" with whom his son consorts. Falstaff urgently pleads on his own behalf—"Banish not him thy Harry's company, banish not him thy Harry's company. Banish plump Jack and banish all the world"—to which the prince chillingly replies, "I do; I will." The tavern will not be Hal's actual second chance.[16]

Hal plays at an escape from his condition that he cannot and will not actually achieve. As he tells himself from the start, he is committed to faking it. His escapades with his tavern mates are as close as he can come to a life that is not governed by the structural hypocrisy that defines his usurper father's reign, but he can participate in those escapades only by whispering inwardly that he is himself a thoroughgoing hypocrite. "I know you all, and will a while uphold / The unyoked humour of your idleness." Hypocrisy is an inheritance he cannot escape, and the best he can do with it is use what he has learned in the tavern to be, as his father was not, a charismatic leader.[17]

The two parts of *Henry IV* stage Hal's attainment of a successful second chance, an attainment that necessitates a repudiation of Falstaff, the master of delinquency. In the first part, the prince sets aside his idleness and rises to the martial challenge he had been avoiding. When he asks Falstaff for a sword and is offered instead a bottle of sack, Hal flings the bottle angrily at his friend: "What, is it a time to jest and dally now?" In the second part, after Hal has acceded to the throne, the repudiation is crueler and more definitive: "I know thee not, old man. Fall to thy prayers."[18]

The first of these moments is private, occurring between

Hal and Falstaff alone. Hal then returns to battle, where he encounters and kills his rival, Hotspur. Only Falstaff, who is on
the ground playing dead, witnesses that encounter, so he can
later claim that it was he who killed Hotspur after the latter revived and continued to fight. Hal allows Falstaff to get away with
the lie, which in turn allows the drama of delinquency to continue into 2 *Henry IV.* The second repudiation, by contrast, is
fully public and final. It marks the fulfillment of the long-term
plan Hal had revealed in his soliloquy early in part 1. "When
this loose behavior I throw off," he declared,

> And pay the debt I never promisèd,
> By how much better than my word I am,
> By so much shall I falsify men's hopes;
> And, like bright metal on a sullen ground,
> My reformation, glittering o'er my fault,
> Shall show more goodly and attract more eyes
> Than that which hath no foil to set it off.
> I'll so offend to make offense a skill,
> Redeeming time when men think least I will.

Hal makes it clear that for him achieving a second chance—"redeeming time," as he puts it—requires an audience, a public
performance. It is not enough to grow quietly into a new sense
of himself; what he wants and needs is to attract as many eyes
as possible to his glittering reformation. The whole point of his
delinquency is to enhance the glitter when he finally reveals—
by repudiating his former friends—that he is a new man.[19]

The show is a grand success. In the wake of his father's
death, the reformed prince—no longer madcap Hal—has become King Henry V. "My father has gone wild into his grave, / For
in his tomb lie my affections," the new king tells the Lord Chief
Justice,

> And with his spirits sadly I survive
> To mock the expectation of the world,
> To frustrate prophecies, and to raze out
> Rotten opinion, who hath writ me down
> After my seeming.

He has buried his delinquent self along with his father's corpse—indeed the two have merged—and the spirit within him now is his father's. He appears in what he calls "formal majesty," in a solemn procession of nobles and high officials. Against the expectation of the world, he has triumphed. But it is a triumph based, as he had planned from the start, on falsifying men's hopes and on skillful offending. Redemption has come through systematic lying.[20]

There is something quietly devastating about Hal's reformation at the play's close. Doll Tearsheet, who has evidently been Hal's lover as well as Falstaff's, and Mistress Quickly, the owner of the tavern, are arrested for prostitution and will be publicly whipped by the beadles. Their great expectations all dashed, Falstaff, Pistol, and Bardolph are led away to prison. Shakespeare could have darkened the picture still further, but he held off, reserving for a later play, *Henry V,* the revelation that Hal's rejection of Falstaff had fatal consequences: "The King has killed his heart." At the end of *2 Henry IV,* blindsided and humiliated, Falstaff exits trying to assure himself and his friends that the rejection is only for show: "I shall be sent for soon at night." He still thinks that there will be a tomorrow. But it is telling that Shakespeare reserves the play's final words—words praising "this fair proceeding of the King's"—to two of its coldest, least likable characters, the ruthless, humorless Prince John and the harsh, censorious Lord Chief Justice.[21]

Hal's second chance is a victory of cunning barely distinguishable from what his father had all along wanted him to be.

It is in effect the old first chance tricked out as a second chance. As such, it is rhetorically effective, but it bears the distinctly bitter taste of betrayal. It is at once shiny and dirty. "Bright metal on a sullen ground."[22]

Not all second chances, even the most successful of them, are entirely appealing.

With the two *Henry IV* plays, Shakespeare had by no means exhausted his interest in delinquency and second chances. He drew upon it multiple times in different genres, from the dark history play *Richard II* to the bittersweet problem comedy *All's Well That Ends Well,* to the late romance *The Tempest.* His greatest exploration of the subject came in a tragedy, *Antony and Cleopatra.* The hero is not a young man, buying himself some time before he assumes his inherited position in society, but an aging warrior who has long ago proved himself and is not looking for any radical change in his identity. And the delinquency in question is not a cunning career move or a bid for attention. It is the experience of a desire so irresistible, intense, and transformative that it becomes, in spite of Antony's own intentions and at the ultimate cost of his life, his second chance.

The experience was never meant to be anything of the kind. His sometime partner and dangerous rival Octavius Caesar remarks that in Egypt, Antony has "filled / His vacancy with voluptuousness." By "vacancy" Octavius means something like vacation, the time when a person is expected to indulge in leisure activities. In Antony's case, some of these activities resemble Hal's in the tavern:

> to sit
> And keep the turn of tippling with a slave,
> To reel the streets at noon, and stand the buffet
> With knaves that smell of sweat.

But the great general's pleasures extend beyond mingling intimately with those beneath his social rank. To make love to Cleopatra—"To tumble on the bed of Ptolemy," as Caesar puts it—is the principal way Antony fills his idle hours, and not only his idle hours. His indulgence in this "voluptuousness" extends to times that demand his most sustained and energetic attention. This confounding of what is—or should be—merely recreational with what is serious and essential lies at the heart of what Octavius sees as Antony's delinquency, a dereliction of duty unacceptable in a youth and outrageous in a mature adult.[23]

Antony entirely agrees. "These strong Egyptian fetters I must break, / Or lose myself in dotage." "I must from this enchanting queen break off." "I must with haste from hence." "I must be gone." "I'll leave you, lady." But breaking off turns out to be far more difficult than he ever imagined it would be. The whole play is about his inability to leave the lady, and that inability has everything to do with the character of Cleopatra, one of Shakespeare's most astonishing creations.[24]

In her irresistible power to provoke delinquency, Cleopatra bears an odd, surprising resemblance to Falstaff. To be sure, one is an imperious queen, the other a down-at-heels scoundrel; one the emblem of everything that the early seventeenth century found exotic, the other a flamboyant version of the familiar drunkard at the corner tavern; one a figure of infinite erotic allure, the other a wheezing, perspiring mountain of flesh. What they share is an overwhelming intensity of life that makes time spent in their company seem more exciting, delightful, playful, gratifying, joyful, and purely pleasurable than time spent anywhere else with anyone else.

Falstaff and Cleopatra are alike in seeing with utmost clarity what the person they wish to charm most needs and craves. Like Hal, Antony is drawn to truancy, but it is a different kind of truancy, one that is anything but calculated or strategic. From the perspective of the Roman world, Antony's delinquency is merely an ominous sign of his getting soft—what the first line of the play calls "dotage." Rome is associated with efficiency, rational calculation, and speed; Egypt with levity, extravagance, and idleness. Antony's Egyptian sojourn is career disaster. The last thing that a battle-worn general jockeying with a ruthless youthful rival needs is to absent himself from the center of power.

But absenting himself from the center is precisely what Antony seems to want. By saying that Antony "filled / His vacancy with voluptuousness," Octavius may mean only to impugn his rival's waste of vacation time, but the striking phrase suggests something else, something deeper. For Antony the center—the center of Rome, the center of his brilliantly successful career, the center perhaps of his own being—has come to seem as pallid and hollow as Octavia, the prim, dutiful, uninteresting sister of Caesar whom he marries in a last-ditch attempt to patch up the rift that threatens to erupt in civil war. What Antony seeks to fill his vacancy is what Cleopatra offers him, and all that has hitherto anchored his life seems to him expendable or evanescent. "Let Rome in Tiber melt," he declares, embracing the Egyptian queen, "and the wide arch / Of the ranged empire fall. . . . / There's not a minute of our lives should stretch / Without some pleasure now."[25]

The pleasure Antony seeks, and for which he is willing to give up everything, has nothing to do with an imagined future. It is all about the present, the current minute stretched out or slowed down to an intimation of limitlessness. That this oceanic sense entails loss—"Let Rome in Tiber melt"—does not matter, or perhaps the loss, painful though it is, is part of the pleasure. Enobarbus's celebrated description of Cleopatra's first appearance before Antony is lifted in most of its details from Plutarch's masterful *Life of Marcus Antonius* (ca. 110 CE), but

Shakespeare adds several telling variations on his source. Plutarch mentions "the oars of silver, which kept stroke in rowing after the sound of the music of flutes"; in Shakespeare

> the oars were silver,
> Which to the tune of flutes kept stroke, and made
> The water which they beat to follow faster,
> As amorous of their strokes.

The image of the water aroused by being beaten glances slyly at the way Antony's pleasure is intensified by what seems to frustrate him or cause him pain.[26]

Cleopatra is fully conscious of this effect. "If you find him sad, / Say I am dancing," she tells a go-between; "if in mirth, report / That I am sudden sick." When one of her attendants urges her instead, "in each thing give him way," she replies sharply, "Thou teachest like a fool, the way to lose him." He is drawn toward what crosses him.[27]

The losses are not merely symbolic, nor is the pain simply playful. "Ten thousand harms more than the ills I know / My idleness doth hatch," Antony anxiously berates himself, early in the play, and his anxieties prove entirely well founded. When, after repairing some of the damage caused by his truancy, he cannot resist returning to Egypt— "I' th' East my pleasure lies"—he fractures the fragile alliance that had prevented Rome from descending into civil war. And when, after Cleopatra and her fleet have fled from the decisive sea battle, he turns and follows her, he seals his fate. "She once being loofed," a horrified observer reports,

> The noble ruin of her magic, Antony,
> Claps on his sea-wing, and—like a doting mallard—
> Leaving the fight in height, flies after her![28]

"The noble ruin of her magic"—Antony's pursuit of his own destruction is the culmination of the pattern already glimpsed in the water that seems amorous of the strokes that beat it. For the observer, who is one of Antony's staunch friends and allies, the disaster strikes at core Roman values, values that Antony had once supremely embodied:

> I never saw an action of such shame.
> Experience, manhood, honor ne'er before
> Did violate so itself.

Antony would not disagree: "I have fled myself," he says; "Authority melts from me." Yet Shakespeare's great tragedy manages to suggest that Antony has not only lost his martial identity—the first chance that he had developed over the years and that had made him a towering Roman hero—but has also, against all odds and through his very delinquency, achieved a new identity, a second chance. That identity is defined by love, not valor, but it is a love very different from the fresh, single-minded passion that drives the characters of the comedies, young men and women in the grip of ardent idealizations. Antony has had ample time and occasion to become thoroughly disillusioned with Cleopatra. He takes in, not once but multiple times, her theatricality, her manipulative tricks, her promiscuity, her fraudulence. "I found you," he says bitterly,

> as a morsel cold upon
> Dead Caesar's trencher. Nay, you were a fragment
> Of Gneius Pompey's—besides what hotter hours
> Unregistered in vulgar fame you have
> Luxuriously picked out.

In the heat of anger, things are sometimes said that cannot be unsaid and that mark the end of a relationship. This would seem to be one of those moments, and yet for Antony and Cleopatra it is not the end, at least not yet. Their decisions have led to a succession of disasters and to the utter ruin that now impends. On both their parts there is disillusionment, no end of disillusionment. But somehow the disillusionment is part of their bond. Their love recovers, endures, renews itself. "Let's have one other gaudy night," Antony says; "Come on, my queen, / There's sap in't yet."[29]

At this life-or-death juncture, Antony opts to redouble his delinquency. How is it that he would choose sexual desire over survival itself? The answer certainly does not depend on the planning of a family or indeed on any planning at all. It is bound up with Antony's identity—that is, with the second chance his delinquency has won him. And Cleopatra declares that her identity is bound up with his: "Since my lord / Is Antony again," she says, after they have reconciled, "I will be Cleopatra." It is impossible to determine what lies behind this theatrical self-representation. Both Antony and Cleopatra are constantly playing themselves. Without their self-fashioning—the ceaseless rhetorical display and enactment of what it is to be Antony and Cleopatra—there would be no identity and little desire. Their desire dwells almost entirely in representation, which is why for them eros can outlive youth, can outlive the body's beauty, can outlive life itself.[30]

Not all second chances are in the service of survival. Antony's desire for Cleopatra has always implied the death of his Roman self. His friends have grasped this from the beginning, and he himself has intermittently seen it coming. His Egyptian truancy has all along been a drive toward death. It is not surprising, then, that, upon being told that Cleopatra is dead, his ultimate performance of desire is an eroticized suicide attempt:

> I will be
> A bridegroom in my death, and run into 't
> As to a lover's bed.

The suicide attempt is botched, which gives the dying Antony time to understand that once again Cleopatra has deceived him and to perform for a final time the renewal of his desire through pain:

> I am dying, Egypt, dying. Only
> I here importune death awhile until
> Of many thousand kisses the poor last
> I lay upon thy lips.[31]

The surprise at the end of the tragedy is that Cleopatra embraces Antony's second chance: she too commits suicide. She did not seem to have experienced a comparable transformation of her identity. On the contrary, she had, as Antony observed, been attached to a succession of powerful Roman generals before him. Understanding this perfectly well, in his dying words he urges her to turn now to the triumphant Octavius Caesar. Instead, renouncing the pattern of her life and declaring, "Husband, I come," she puts the asp to her breast. Would she have done so had she not been informed what Octavius had in store for her is not clear; nothing about Cleopatra's motivations is ever entirely clear. But she too manages to fashion death as her second chance.[32]

4

Shakespeare's Second Chance

B y the time William Shakespeare reached the age of twenty-one, he had a wife and three children. And then he abandoned them, leaving them in a provincial market town and heading off to the capital to pursue—well, whatever it was that at that point in his life he imagined he was going to do. True, after he established himself as an actor and writer and entrepreneur, he returned from London from time to time, presumably to see his wife and children, along with his aging parents. And as his wealth increased, he sent money back to Stratford-upon-Avon, resettled his family in a large house, and made a succession of local real estate and commodity investments. To that extent he remained connected. But it is telling that there were no more children born to Anne and Will, nor is there any evidence that the busy playwright shared his rich inner world with his wife, or that he involved himself in the lives of his two daughters and his son, or that anyone in his family was able to read or write with even moderate facility.

Surviving documents suggest that other actors who came from the provinces brought their families to London and settled them there; not so Shakespeare. And if the sonnets have any autobiographical truth to them, his intense emotional and sexual interests lay outside the bounds of his marriage. Between the family in the house on Henley Street in Stratford and the poet in his rented rooms on Silver Street in London, there seems to have been an almost unbridgeable distance.

Biographers presume that Shakespeare rushed home in 1596 for the burial of his eleven-year-old son Hamnet, but this is by no means certain. The boy died in August and Stratford was a two-day ride from London, so it is possible that when word reached the playwright it was already too late. Had there been any warning signs? Did he get the news by letter? Or did someone speak some such words as Shakespeare penned years later in a brief, unbearably painful exchange in *The Winter's Tale*: "Your son . . . is gone." "How, 'gone'?" "Is dead."[1]

It is all the more striking that around 1610, still immensely creative and engaged in all aspects of his profession, the forty-six-year-old Shakespeare seems to have made up his mind to leave London and return to Stratford. It may have taken him some time to extricate himself from his extremely busy life— he was a shareholder in the playing company, the King's Men, as well as its principal playwright and part owner of both of the theaters in which they performed—but by 1611 or 1612 at the latest he was back where he began. Why and in what spirit he reentered the household and resumed life in the place he had turned away from for so many years is unclear. He was hardly recovering his first chance, in the manner of his comic characters. Shakespeare's parents were both dead. His only son was dead. A few of his old friends, like Hamnet and Judith Sadler (after whom the Shakespeares named their twins), were still around, but the close associates, the tavern friends and rivals, the lovers and ex-lovers with whom he had spent the past quarter-century were in London. He had almost completely missed out on the childhood years of both his daughters. The elder, Susanna, had married a prosperous Stratford physician in 1608, moved to his house, and had a baby girl; the younger, Judith, in her mid-twenties, was still at home, along with his wife, Anne, eight years his senior. The curtain is tightly drawn on exactly how they all adjusted to the reconstituted family, and at this point, four hundred years later, it is unlikely to part.

What we do know is that in 1610, Shakespeare decided to write a play about a forty-six-year-old man who recovers a wife and a daughter whom he had deeply injured and whom he believed he had irrevocably lost. Shakespeare did not make up the story out of fragments of his own life. He turned to a best-selling novella, *Pandosto: The Triumph of Time,* written many years earlier by Robert Greene. On his deathbed in 1592, Greene had accused the young Shakespeare, then near the beginning of his career, of being something of a plagiarist—"an upstart crow, beautified with our feathers"—and now, near the end of his career, Shakespeare insouciantly lifted almost the entire plot from his old nemesis.[2]

The setting is the ancient world. Leontes, the king of Sicilia, and his wife, Hermione, who is nearing the term of her pregnancy, have been enjoying a lengthy visit from Leontes' childhood friend Polixenes, the king of Bohemia. Polixenes announces his intention of departing—he says that he needs to attend to responsibilities at home, and besides, he longs to see his young son, something his hosts, who also have a young son, should understand. But Leontes urges him to remain a bit longer—it is as if he cannot bear to let his friend go—and, when his urging fails, tells his wife that she should add her own persuasions. Hermione's efforts are successful, and Polixenes reluctantly but graciously agrees to extend his stay.

This success triggers in Leontes a sudden eruption of violent jealousy. The eruption seems to come from nowhere, like a random, malevolent mutation. Everything is fine—until it is not fine. "They were trained together in their childhoods, and there rooted betwixt them then such an affection which cannot choose but branch now." It is all confident, light, and ebullient— "Tongue-tied, our queen? Speak you"—and then suddenly it is not:

> Too hot, too hot.
> To mingle friendship far is mingling bloods.
> I have *tremor cordis* on me; my heart dances,
> But not for joy, not joy.[3]

Shakespeare's image here is partly medical: one moment you have a perfectly normal heartbeat and the next you are suffering from arrhythmia, *tremor cordis*. The onset was from one beat to the next, but, as with any medical crisis, the etiology inevitably leads back in time. His best friend has been visiting as his houseguest for the past nine months; there must have been innumerable conversations, many of them intimate. But Leontes suddenly sees his wife's brief exchange of words with the friend as raw sex: "To mingle friendship far is mingling bloods." He may not have heard what they were saying, but, as it happens, the mingling of friendship that he was observing with such alarm was a conversation about sex.

In response to a question from Hermione, Polixenes characterizes his boyhood friendship with Leontes as sexless—

> We were as twinned lambs that did frisk i' th' sun
> And bleat the one at th' other. What we changed
> Was innocence for innocence

—and awkwardly contrasts that prelapsarian friendship with the fallen sexual relationships the two men now have with their respective wives. If we hope to understand the sudden eruption of *tremor cordis,* Shakespeare suggests, we need to listen carefully to this conversation about their early childhood. The crisis may occur suddenly, but it almost certainly comes as the consequence of a slow cracking or gradual crumbling. Something disturbing must have already been lingering in the shadows and making itself dimly felt, even over an extended period of time. This lingering disturbance may not have produced any conscious discomfort, but once it comes to consciousness, the past, however reassuringly ordinary it had seemed, now appears in a new and terrible light. All of the once familiar features are defamiliarized.[4]

Leontes himself had instigated the conversation between Hermione and Polixenes. No sly villain has subtly suggested that something improper has been going on. Yet Leontes is seized with an absolute, unshakable certainty. He is convinced that his wife and his best friend, the man he calls his brother, have been having an affair and that the child she is carrying is Polixenes' and not his own.

This certainty is unbearably painful. He can find no way to learn to live with it or to imagine an eventual restoration of the love he had felt. The smallest signs of easy friendship between Hermione and Polixenes are now bitter confirmations of Leontes' fixation. He is well aware that he had long complacently observed and even welcomed these same signs, but his new knowledge—or rather his unshakable certainty—has turned them into poison. His image for this transmutation draws upon the Renaissance belief that a spider consumed with food or drink would be poisonous only if its presence were known to the consumer. But anyone who has glimpsed half a worm in a half-eaten apple will, in any case, easily grasp what he feels:

> There may be in the cup
> A spider steeped, and one may drink, depart,

And yet partake no venom, for his knowledge
Is not infected. But if one present
Th' abhorred ingredient to his eye, make known
How he hath drunk, he cracks his gorge, his sides
With violent hefts.

His knowledge now infected—"I have drunk and seen the spider"—Leontes is seized with nausea.[5]

The physical symptoms that accompany Leontes' delusional certainty—*this* is what has been going on; *this* is what my life was actually like—urgently cry out for relief. Shakespeare's recurrent image for this urgency is vomiting; he desperately wants to get whatever it is out of his system. But the poison is in the mind, not in the stomach; it is not something that has been literally swallowed but something that has finally been seen, something that has at last been made known. Once a life is experienced as a failed first chance, it is impossible to return to a normal state, impossible to put what you now know or think you know out of your mind.

The consequence is a total narrowing of his existence onto this one horrible feeling and a compulsive desire to rid himself of it at any cost. Leontes confides in his chief counselor, Camillo, with words that would in almost all ordinary circumstances be unspeakable: "My wife is slippery." Perceiving at once that the ruler must be seriously ill and that the accusation is untrue, Camillo tries to counter it. "Be cured / Of this diseased opinion," he pleads, "For 'tis most dangerous." But though he is repeatedly given the chance to back off from a charge that is at once a slander to his wife and a humiliation to himself, Leontes insists upon it again and again: "My wife's a hobby-horse"; she "deserves a name / As rank as any flax-wench that puts to / Before her troth plight"; "Were my wife's liver / Infected as her life, she would not live / The running of one glass"; "she's an adulteress"; "she's a traitor"; "she's a bed-swerver." Leontes' whole mental world has been reduced to this one thought, and though the thought is excruciating, he cannot let it go. Indeed he becomes enraged at anyone who tries to tell him the truth:

> You lie, you lie.
> I say thou liest, Camillo, and I hate thee,
> Pronounce thee a gross lout, a mindless slave.[6]

Why should anyone hold on tenaciously to something unbearably painful? Why does Leontes so fiercely refuse every opportunity to reenter the capacious, sunlit world he has lost, to return to trust and love, to be cured? The answer must be that the cure seems worse than the disease, but how is that possible? In words that tumble into incoherence, Leontes tries desperately to articulate to himself how his wife has succumbed, as he imagines it, to her illicit "affection"—that is, her desire. The account tells us nothing about Hermione, but it tells us a great deal about what is happening in his own head:

> Affection, thy intention stabs the center;
> Thou dost make possible things not so held,
> Communicat'st with dreams—how can this be?—
> With what's unreal thou coactive art,
> And fellow'st nothing. Then 'tis very credent
> Thou mayst cojoin with something, and thou dost,
> And that beyond commission, and I find it,
> And that to the infection of my brains
> And hard'ning of my brows.

Desires which traffic in unrealities and communicate with dreams also reach out toward real things and real people in the world. If he has had a vivid fantasy that his wife and his friend are having sex, Leontes tells himself, indeed *because* he has had this fantasy, then it stands to reason—it is "very credent"—that it is happening in reality. Later in the play, denying the charge of adultery, Hermione says to Leontes, "You speak a language that I understand not. / My life stands in the level of your dreams." He replies, "Your actions are my dreams." Presumably he means to suggest that what she is calling his mere dreams are her actual actions, but his words seem only to confirm his perverse, destructive insistence on his own fantasy, his insistence that his fantasy must be true.[7]

But how to account for this determination to shout, "I am right, I am right, I am right," not only when everyone swears that he is wrong but also when the insistence causes him so much pain? Leontes is fully aware of the suffering he is causing himself: "Dost think I am so muddy, so unsettled," he asks Camillo, "To appoint myself in this vexation?" The pain radiates out to his beloved son, whose legitimate birth, though Leontes himself does not doubt it, will inevitably be called into question. Would I then, he continues,

> Sully the purity and whiteness of my sheets—
> Which to preserve is sleep, which being spotted
> Is goads, thorns, nettles, tails of wasps—
> Give scandal to the blood o' th' prince, my son,
> Who I do think is mine and love as mine,
> Without ripe moving to 't? Would I do this?

Leontes' questions are meant to be rhetorical, but what the underlying motive—the "ripe moving to 't"—actually is remains maddeningly unclear.[8]

What is clear is that absolutely no one can make Leontes doubt his settled belief. "You may as well / Forbid the sea for to obey the moon," Camillo observes,

As or by oath remove or counsel shake
The fabric of his folly, whose foundation
Is piled upon his faith and will continue
The standing of his body.

Folly built on a foundation of faith does not amount to a motive, but it does get at the way Leontes clings to his mad certainty as if his life and the universe itself depended on it. "Is
this nothing?" he says, when Camillo calls his supposed proof
in doubt,

Why, then, the world and all that's in't is nothing,
The covering sky is nothing, Bohemia nothing,
My wife is nothing, nor nothing have these nothings
If this be nothing.

These are the accents of faith, the faith the true believers live
and die for.[9]

Or in Leontes' case—as in the case of so many other true
believers—kill for. Incapable of questioning himself and refusing all proffered opportunities for a second chance, Leontes
orders Camillo to poison Polixenes. Camillo, unwilling to carry
out the order, warns Polixenes, and together they make their
escape from Sicilia.

This escape does not awaken a rethinking or provide Leontes with a second chance; it only confirms him in his worst
suspicions. In Shakespeare's account a person whose world is
falling apart tries desperately to distinguish between things
that are beyond his grasp and those that he can do something
about. In Leontes' case, his treacherous friend has escaped from
Sicilia and is now safely back in his own kingdom. The "harlot
king," Leontes acknowledges, "Is quite beyond mine arm, out
of the blank / And level of my brain." There is nothing to be

done about him. But not so his adulterous wife: "Say that she were gone," he muses, "Given to the fire, a moiety of my rest / Might come to me again."[10]

Along with nausea and murderous rage, then, is another symptom: sleeplessness. "Nor night nor day," Leontes says, "no rest." He reproaches himself for his insomnia, as if it were a personal failure: "It is but weakness / To bear the matter thus, mere weakness." But being angry at himself for not sleeping is no help. He cannot sleep because he is afraid of what he might dream—"Your actions are my dreams"—and because at all costs he needs to stay awake. Leontes thinks that for nine months he has been asleep, while his wife and his friend were having an affair and while everyone in his court has been whispering about it. His insomnia now is as much a desperate self-cure as it is a symptom: how could he possibly sleep now that finally he knows what has been going on? But the insomnia, like the nausea and the rage, only ensures that he is farther away than ever from a return to inner peace and the recovery of joy. Leontes' self-cure is relentless self-sabotage.[11]

The phenomenon that *The Winter's Tale* dramatizes with such intensity lies at the heart of Freud's thought. Psychoanalysis, which began as a cure for neurosis, quickly became an attempt to explain and address the sheer scale of people's self-destructiveness. The "negative therapeutic reaction" Freud termed what he repeatedly observed: patients came for psychoanalysis claiming to want to change while unconsciously working very hard to hold on to their suffering. It was not simply that people were tempted to act against their own best interests but that often they actually hated and attacked their own well-being. What Freud would eventually refer to as the "death instinct" was the part of the self that sabotaged the self's aliveness and vitality.[12]

Freud described people as essentially and inventively self-sabotaging, as though the pressures of life, both internal and

external, were somehow excessive and unbearable. While people often claimed to want for themselves what Nietzsche called
more life, they were actually driven to create less life. More particularly, they were adept at creating, as Macbeth or Leontes do,
a life they could only loathe. They unconsciously preferred and
sought out a kind of death-in-life.

"Dost think I am so muddy, so unsettled," Leontes asks,
"To appoint myself in this vexation?" Shakespeare's answer, like
Freud's, is that yes, he is precisely so unsettled and yes, he has
set about to destroy his own happiness. But why? In *Macbeth*
and *Othello*, there are malevolent agents, the witches and the
villainous Iago, to whom the blame can rightly or wrongly be
assigned, but *The Winter's Tale* has no such agent. At the height
of his happiness, with a loving wife and a thriving family, and
in the company of his best friend, Leontes is compelled to wreck
it all. Shakespeare does not offer an explanation for this compulsion; perhaps he did not have one, or perhaps he preferred
to leave the speculation to his audience.[13]

Freud and his followers do offer an explanation. The experience of pleasure, they theorized, awakens the fear of being
overwhelmed by desire, the threat, as the psychoanalyst Jean
Laplanche put it, of "the attack of the drives on the ego."[14] Moreover, enjoying oneself always carries the risk, at its most minimal, of making one dangerously dependent on the source of one's
enjoyment. To this risk is added the possibility of arousing envy
in others; and, as a final insult, a part of the self, the so-called
death instinct, wants us to suffer and die. Self-destructiveness—
the compulsion to do the self-harming, devastating thing, so
powerfully displayed in Leontes—is the course that a great
many people assiduously follow.

Leontes is offered multiple opportunities to be healed,
and he cannot or will not take any of them. He is told again and
again by the people in his world he has most reason to trust

that his suspicions are groundless. He has had ample confirmation over many years of the love of his wife and his friend. He has a promising young son and heir whose striking resemblance to himself everyone recognizes. Yet he clings fiercely to hateful thoughts that inflict pain upon himself—or perhaps we should say that those thoughts cling fiercely to him. He cannot shake them off. Even after he has made his charges public and brought humiliation upon his whole family, he is given the chance to repudiate his accusation and seize upon the chance for renewed love, but he refuses to do so. He shuts himself off from all who wish to help him, all whose skeptical, caring words of advice offer to free him from his terrible illusion. The suffering he gets from his continued humiliation is somehow preferable to the suffering he fears he would get without the vindication— the justice, as he imagines it—that he demands.

Leontes publicly accuses Hermione of adultery, a charge of high treason punishable by death. To put on trial and execute the person one thinks has caused one's misery is the special prerogative of kings. (Shakespeare and his contemporaries had from the recent past the reign of Henry VIII to contemplate.) But when things fall apart, it is not only rulers who experience rage. Fantasies of revenge are part of the experience of losing something that had seemed like a secure possession. Though they are unlikely to deliver the relief they promise—to give Leontes a "moiety" of his rest, say, four hours of sleep a night—they offer a temporary, local satisfaction, like scratching an itch. But like scratching an itch, they almost always cause more pain than they relieve.

Rage, as Shakespeare's play makes clear, works to deflect any sense of responsibility from the self, and it invariably strikes more than its intended object. Anxiously observing the declining health of his young son, Leontes understands that the ill-

ness is a consequence of the marital crisis, but he holds to account his wife, not himself:

> Conceiving the dishonor of his mother,
> He straight declined, drooped, took it deeply,
> Fastened and fixed the shame on't in himself,
> Threw off his spirit, his appetite, his sleep,
> And downright languished.[15]

It is *her* dishonor that has harmed the boy, not his own
fastening and fixing of shame upon her. Shakespeare manages
to capture the way in which parents locked in ferocious marital arguments use children as pawns and objects of competitive identification:

> Give me the boy; I am glad you did not nurse him.
> Though he does bear some signs of me, yet you
> Have too much blood in him.

Contemptuously dismissing Hermione's fervent denials of guilt
and separating her from their son, he imprisons her while she
awaits a trial whose conclusion is foregone. Leontes rebuffs the
pleas of his counselors, though to mitigate the appearance of
arbitrariness he sends two messengers to consult the oracle in
Apollo's temple in what the play calls Delphos.[16]

In prison Hermione gives birth to a girl. Her devoted
friend Paulina decides to show the newborn to Leontes. Tormented by sleeplessness and anxiety for his son, who has been
ailing since the charges were leveled against Hermione, Leontes has refused to receive anyone, but the outspoken Paulina
insists on entering. She urges him to perceive that the features
of the newborn's face resemble his own and to withdraw his

unjust accusation, but her intervention only further enrages him. He commands that the baby be immediately killed. When the horrified counselors plead for mercy, he orders Paulina's husband, Antigonus, to take it to a remote shore and abandon it to its fate.

With Leontes as both accuser and judge, the treason trial proceeds. As it nears its foreordained end, the messengers return, and the sealed oracle they have brought with them is opened and read aloud. The Delphic oracle was famously ambiguous, but for once its words are unequivocal: "Hermione is chaste, Polixenes blameless, Camillo a true subject, Leontes a jealous tyrant, his innocent babe truly begotten; and the King shall live without an heir if that which is lost be not found."[17] Leontes declares that the oracle is false. But as the trial resumes at his insistence, word is brought him that his son has died. The grief-stricken king immediately declares that the heavens are punishing him for his injustice. Hermione collapses and is carried off; Paulina returns a few moments later with the news that she too has died. Leontes declares that he will bury the mother and son in one grave, which he will visit daily as long as he lives.

The remainder of the play shifts radically not only in setting—from Sicilia to Bohemia and from court to country—but also in form. A taut courtroom drama with a tragic outcome gives way to the wild improbabilities of literary romance. Following Leontes' orders, the baby is abandoned on a remote seacoast by Antigonus, who promptly meets his end in the wake of Shakespeare's most notorious stage direction: "*Exit, pursued by a bear*."[18] The baby is found and adopted by a shepherd. Sixteen years pass. The little foundling, named Perdita, has grown into a beautiful young woman. She is wooed by a young man who claims to be a shepherd but turns out to be none other than Prince Florizel, the son and heir of Polixenes. A series of

zany twists and turns leads Perdita and Florizel to flee from
the irate father to Sicilia, where they are welcomed by Leontes.
Polixenes, accompanied by Camillo, soon follows, determined
to prevent what he regards as the catastrophic marriage between his son and a peasant girl. But the girl is disclosed through
certain signs preserved from her swaddling clothes to be the
lost princess. Leontes and his daughter are joyously reunited;
so too are Leontes and his estranged friend Polixenes.

A final surprise awaits. Paulina invites everyone to her
garden house to see a lifelike statue of Hermione that she has
specially commissioned. The observers are stunned when the
figure breathes, descends from the pedestal, and embraces her
husband and daughter. The three are miraculously reunited.
The family—all but the dead son—will have a second chance
in life.

It will not do to line up *The Winter's Tale* neatly with
Shakespeare's life. The plot was lifted from someone else, and
besides, it is far more like a daydream than a depiction of reality. Indeed, as the title itself suggests, it is explicitly marked out
in multiple ways as a tale or fantasy: the statue that comes to
life is only the most extreme instance. Among the relatively
few changes that Shakespeare made to Greene's plot was to flip
the locations in order to give landlocked Bohemia a seacoast,
as if he were laughing at the absurdity of it all. As a character near
the end of the play remarks, "This news which is called true is
so like an old tale that the verity of it is in strong suspicion."[19]

But fantasies, as Freud supremely understood, are often
more revealing than sober reports, and art, as Shakespeare supremely understood, exists as a way to enable us to enter into
someone else's fantasy and make it our own. There is, in any
case, something striking in Shakespeare's engagement at this
moment of his life with Greene's story, a story in which a father,
haunted by a painful sense of guilt for the death of his only son,

is reunited years later with the daughter whom he had cast away as an infant. And it is still more striking that, taking this story over from Greene, Shakespeare made one huge change. He radically rewrote its ending so as to give the wayward husband the opportunity to repair his damaged relationship with his wife. At the close of *Pandosto,* there is no going back: the wife is dead, along with the little boy, and the husband and father, tormented by guilt, kills himself. At the close of *The Winter's Tale,* by contrast, Shakespeare offers the astonishing possibility of a second chance.

The Winter's Tale seems designed to serve as a template for understanding the idea of a second chance in life. This is, of course, independent of whether Shakespeare succeeded in having one of his own. His premature death at the age of fifty-two, only a few years after he returned to Stratford, gave him very little time to heal wounds, assuming there were wounds to heal, and to rebuild trust. But we know that his imagination had long dwelt on the possibility of recovering what had seemed irrevocably lost, of returning to circumstances that had passed and replaying them all with different results, of undoing catastrophic mistakes and—in Prince Hal's words from *1 Henry IV*—"redeeming time."[20] This brooding is evident not only from the changes Shakespeare made to the plot he lifted late in his career from Greene but also, as we saw in *Julius Caesar, King Lear,* and *Othello,* from several strange and resonant moments in some of his most celebrated tragedies.

The Winter's Tale unfolds a scenario loosely similar to the one that opens *Lear*: a rash, tyrannical father condemns his daughter to death. To be sure, Lear's daughter Cordelia is a young adult, not a newborn, and her father does not order her execution but merely sends her off with his curse. But he makes clear that he cancels out her existence—"Better thou had'st / Not been born than not t' have pleased me better"—and her terrible fate is a consequence of his rage. Leontes' rage comparably reduces his daughter to a thing, an "it" he wants destroyed: "Take it hence," he orders, "And see it instantly consumed with fire." When his words meet resistance from his courtiers, he reiterates the order, along with a stern warning:

> If thou refuse,
> And wilt encounter with my wrath, say so.
> The bastard brains with these my proper hands
> Shall I dash out. Go, take it to the fire.

Only after further pleading does he slightly mitigate his command, ordering instead that it be brought to some remote and desert place and abandoned "without more mercy." As the man charged with this deed grimly remarks, "A present death / Had been more merciful." Shakespeare goes out of his way then to emphasize Leontes' murderous cruelty, in comparison to which Lear's act of disowning and cursing his daughter was positively mild. But in spite of it all, in *The Winter's Tale* the father gets his daughter back.[21]

In staging this unexpected recovery Shakespeare was closely following his source, *Pandosto*. In Greene's story, as in the play, a powerful ruler falls into the grip of a conviction that his pregnant wife has had an affair with his best friend. Pandosto has more cause than Leontes to be suspicious. There grew between the wife and the friend, Greene writes, such mutual admiration and "such a secret uniting of their affections that the one could not well be without the company of the other." The husband's violent jealousy leads him to an attempt on his friend's life and, when the friend flees, to a public accusation of adultery against his wife. Not only does he put his innocent wife on trial, he also casts away his newborn daughter, whom he believes is illegitimate. Only when his young son, deeply affected by his mother's fate, sickens and dies does the shock of the loss bring the insane man to his senses. Apollo's oracle, solicited to adjudicate the case, declares that "the King shall live without an heir if that which is lost be not found"—Shakespeare lifted the words verbatim from Greene—but by then it seems to be too late: his wife has collapsed and died, and his daughter has been consigned to an almost certain death.[22]

Of course, as we would expect in a romance, that which is lost is found—the abandoned infant survives and, sixteen years later, now a beautiful young woman, she appears as a stranger in her father's kingdom. The father does not recognize his daughter. After all, how could he, having cast her away as a newborn sixteen years earlier? In Greene this nonrecognition leads to disaster: the king is sexually aroused by the lovely creature newly arrived in his kingdom and does everything he can to seduce her. Eventually, when the mystery of her identity is solved, he is initially filled with joy: "I am thy father!" But the elation soon gives way to what Greene calls "desperate thoughts," that is, his realization that in addition to having betrayed his friend and his wife, he has now committed yet another crime: "contrary to the law of nature, he had lusted after his own daughter." The combined weight of what he has done and what he now feels drives him to suicide. It is with this act—"to close up the comedy with a tragical stratagem," as Greene puts it—that the novella ends.[23]

In Shakespeare too a moment comes in which the king finds himself sexually attracted to the beautiful young woman whom he does not yet recognize to be his lost daughter Perdita. But his arousal is immediately countered by Paulina, who has assumed the role of his spiritual adviser, the critic to whose voice he must always listen:

> Sir, my liege,
> Your eye hath too much youth in 't. Not a month
> 'Fore your queen died, she was more worth such gazes
> Than what you look on now.

"Your eye hath too much youth in 't": you are too old, she tells him, to be interested in such a young girl, and besides, even nine months pregnant his wife was more beautiful than she.[24] Leontes' response is enigmatic:

> I thought of her
> Even in these looks I made.

Perhaps he is acknowledging the justice of Paulina's words: the memory of the woman whom his jealousy had destroyed came to him as a reproach just as for an instant he was attracted to someone else. But perhaps he is saying something different: looking at the features of the beautiful young stranger, he thought of his dead wife, and that thought allowed him for an instant to feel something that he had not felt for sixteen penitential years. He is awakening to the possibility of a second chance. But a new life with a much younger woman is not the outcome that Paulina—or *The Winter's Tale*—has in mind for Leontes.[25]

In ordering the destruction of his daughter, Leontes resembles Lear, but in his central, soul-destroying preoccupation with jealousy, he is far closer to Othello, who is led by his tormenting suspicion to smother his wife. Othello was given the possibility of a second chance, but it came in a poisoned form by the demonic "honest" Iago, who suggests at one point that Othello simply live with Desdemona's faithlessness, accepting it as the way things are, the way all woman are. After all, Iago remarks wryly, the wine she drinks is made of grapes. Leontes has a momentary thought of a similar kind—everyone is betrayed by "Sir Smile," who fishes in his neighbor's pond. But these thoughts, this form of disillusionment, attack the very foundation of identity. Both Othello and Leontes would rather murder the women they have loved than accept such a terrible possibility.

In *The Winter's Tale* Shakespeare almost seems to have wanted to conduct a wild experiment: what if Othello had not committed suicide, as he does in the tragedy that bears his name, but instead, after many years of misery and repentance, discovered that Desdemona had survived? What if he were freed from his suspicion and cured of his murderous misogyny? What if Othello were granted a second chance at the marriage he had wrecked?

Shakespeare's experiment is stranger still, for even in his madness Othello never entirely loses his innate nobility, his craving for justice, and his instinct for openness. Leontes is far worse: he secretly plots to poison his best friend and, running roughshod over the most basic canons of human decency and law, behaves like a merciless tyrant. He makes every effort to murder a newborn baby; his cruelty leads to the death of his son; after a disgusting show trial, he orders the execution of his wife, whom even a divine oracle has declared innocent. Unlike Othello, he does all these things without the instigation of a villain. So it is as if Shakespeare took Othello, folded him together with Iago, threw in something of the viciousness of Richard III, and then set himself the task of giving this hopeless case a second chance. Small wonder that Shakespeare's rival Ben Jonson made a snide remark about *The Winter's Tale*. He thought that Shakespeare was violating decorum, decency, and common sense—making nature, as Jonson put it, afraid.

In *The Winter's Tale* Shakespeare was not interested in constructing a plausible plot; he was interested in exploring the psychological stages that could follow from an act of radi-

cal self-destructiveness and lead eventually to the possibility
of some form of recovery. With his world falling apart, Leontes
suffers from a suite of symptoms: *tremor cordis,* nausea, insomnia, and rage. It is only after his son dies that an emotion fully
surfaces in him that is closely linked to rage, namely, grief. The
two emotions can be experienced together, but Shakespeare
decouples them in order to emphasize the blinding intensity of
the former, an intensity that suppresses the expression of anything else. Indeed, even after the terrible news of his son's death
has shattered his rage and finally made him acknowledge the
injustice of his charges, Leontes does not seem entirely to register all that he has lost.

When he is brought the news of Hermione's collapse,
he expresses confidence that she has only fainted—"She will
recover"—and goes on to envisage the way he will undo the
damage:

> I'll reconcile me to Polixenes,
> New woo my queen, recall the good Camillo,
> Whom I proclaim a man of truth, of mercy.

But these good intentions are a delusion—less the dream of
the second chance than the fantasy that the first can be resumed. Nothing can be so readily repaired. It is only when the
actual state of things is laid out before him by the relentless
Paulina—you have, she tells him, betrayed your friend, attempted to poison the honor of your most trusted adviser, ordered the destruction of your newborn daughter, and caused
the deaths of both your son and your wife—that Leontes, recognizing what he has done, can begin to allow the grief to well
up in him. There is no going forward without such recognition.[26]

Recognition has both an outward and an inward dimension. It is never enough, the play implies, simply to refashion

your inner life without making that refashioning manifest in relationships and gestures, and it is never enough to reframe your behavior without undergoing a comparable reframing of the psyche. The outward dimension of acknowledgment is manifested in certain formal acts. These vary widely depending on the circumstances. They can involve a move from one city or country to another, or a change of occupation, or a new name, or the radical transformation of identity.

In *The Winter's Tale* Leontes determines literally to face what he has done and to declare his guilt to the world:

> Prithee bring me
> To the dead bodies of my queen and son.
> One grave shall be for both. Upon them shall
> The causes of their death appear, unto
> Our shame perpetual.

His responsibility will be inscribed in stone so that his shame can never fade and be forgotten. And at the same time he initiates for himself a ritual observance:

> Once a day I'll visit
> The chapel where they lie, and tears shed there
> Shall be my recreation. So long as nature
> Will bear up with this exercise, so long
> I daily vow to use it.

There is obvious irony in the term "recreation"; daily tears of grief and remorse for the rest of his life will hardly be an agreeable pastime. But there is also an underlying longing for re-creation, a hope that just as the body can be remade through daily exercise, so too his inner life can be remade if it can endure ("bear up with") the burden of the ritual.[27]

Anxiety about bearing up under the psychic and physical stress of loss may have an element of self-pity, but it is not altogether misguided. Experience of the kind that Leontes proposes to undertake can in fact damage health, though not perhaps in the way that he imagines. It is not the daily ritual of weeping that is likely to be harmful; if anything, the weeping might offer some relief. Rather it is what is likely to come in the wake of such a ritual. His wife, Hermione, so much wiser than her husband, describes the dangerous effect upon her of the loss of everything she most valued. Tears are not the problem, she says; she is not "prone to weeping, as our sex / Commonly are." She has lodged within her a grief "which burns / Worse than tears drown." Though it does not show outwardly, this burning has consumed any desire within her to survive. It has made life seem worthless. "To me," she declares, "can life be no commodity." Her numbness gives her a certain moral courage, as she makes clear when Leontes threatens her with execution: "Tell me what blessings I have here alive, / That I should fear to die." But her courage only anticipates her physical collapse. Leontes' initial expectation that she will quickly recover suggests how far he is from understanding the consequences of what he has brought about and hence how far he still is from encountering anything like a second chance.[28]

As *The Winter's Tale* has it, this distance is measured by the passage of sixteen years. Shakespeare makes no attempt to depict the interval. Instead, with jaunty indifference to the neoclassical rules of the theater, he introduces the allegorical figure of Time, replete with wings and hourglass, to recite a set of rhymed couplets—sixteen of them, one for each year—that move the action rapidly forward. Of the existence of Leontes during this period we learn only that his regret is such that "he shuts up himself." The resonant phrase suggests both that he isolates himself from others and that he contracts within himself. He is in a wasteland without any prospect of emerging from it. The months and years that pass evidently bring no significant change in his life, no sign of healing. The interval demarcates, in effect, the passing of an entire generation, measured in the play's world by the transformation of Perdita from infancy to young womanhood. The figure of Time urges the audience to treat this leap "As you had slept between," but something of the same thing could be said of Leontes in relation to his daughter: it is as if he had been asleep through the whole course of her childhood.[29]

But he has not been asleep. The possibility of a second chance depends on something happening, something largely out of sight. Leontes is quite literally out of sight—offstage and unmentioned—through the whole sequence of scenes set in Bohemia. When we finally see him again, his counselors are pleading with him to bring his long ritual of repentance to an end. "Sir, you have done enough," one of them says,

> and have performed
> A saint-like sorrow. No fault could you make
> Which you have not redeemed, indeed, paid down
> More penitence than done trespass.

The image here is of paying a debt: Leontes has incurred a penalty as a result of his transgression, but he has now fully made amends. Indeed he has, according to the counselor, paid down more than he owed, both in the eyes of heaven and in the eyes of his fellow men. There is a long historical tradition of dealing with transgression and loss in this way, through the formal fulfillment of an obligation. It is as if there were a regulated emotional economy: the task is to determine how much you owe for your blunders, to settle up appropriately, and then move on. Another of Leontes' counselors makes still more explicit what moving on would mean. As things stand, the kingdom is endangered "by his highness' fail of issue." Leontes should marry again to replace the wife who has died and produce a new heir to the throne to replace the son and daughter he has lost.[30]

But Leontes counters with a very different image for what he has been going through:

> Whilst I remember
> Her and her virtues, I cannot forget
> My blemishes in them, and so still think of
> The wrong I did myself.

There are two different painful memories here: a memory of lost happiness and a memory of his own blemishes or defects. Those defects have led to the loss of what he possessed—that is, the loss of his first and, as far as he knows, only chance. Hence his focus is no longer only on what he did to his wife and children; it is on "the wrong I did myself." Memory, in effect, rules out the payment model of reparation. Leontes cannot put his failure behind him, as if it were a debt incurred in the past that he has now fulfilled. Remembrance keeps it alive: "I cannot forget."[31]

Leontes is not alone in remembering what he has lost and in excoriating himself for what he has done. He has an adviser, Paulina, who also insists that he face his responsibility for what he has done. If you took something from every living woman, she tells him, and tried to make a perfect one, "she you killed / Would be unparalleled." Her words are meant to be bitter, and they are. "I think so," he replies, repeating the charge in all its severity: "Killed? / She I killed?" And then he adds, "I did so." The three simple words—an unqualified acceptance of direct responsibility—are a crucial part of Leontes' working through his trauma.[32]

The first counselor objects to Paulina's cruelty, but she holds her ground. "You are one of those / Would have him wed again."[33]

For Paulina this option—the active decision to put it all behind him and move on—is unacceptable. In the context of the plot, she presumably knows that Hermione is still alive and is preparing the coup de théâtre of the statue scene. But from the perspective of the second chance, and particularly from the perspective of psychoanalytic practice, her explanation is suggestive: a second chance does not happen in isolation, or only on one's own initiative. It depends on others, on someone guiding you through it and keeping you honest, even at the cost of making you suffer. The courtiers' advice to Leontes that he move on is, Paulina suggests, a violation of the memory of what has been lost and an attempt to replicate what cannot be replicated. In her view, to go out, look for a new wife, and start a second family is a failure of trust in chance and hence a failure to work through the trauma. Leontes cannot and should not forgive himself. Instead he needs to learn to live with his symptoms.

The Winter's Tale is a deliberately broken-backed play. Not only do sixteen years suddenly pass—represented in the most artificial way, like the pages blown off the calendar in old movies—but the scene shifts from Sicilia to Bohemia, bringing with it a whole new cast of characters. There is a wild storm, a shepherd looking for two of his sheep that have been scared off by young "boiled-brains of nineteen and two-and-twenty," a hungry bear, the chance finding of the abandoned baby and precious jewels, and a host of other seemingly random twists and turns. The critical point is the element of accident throughout, an apparently meaningless chain of chance encounters.[34]

These arbitrary encounters will, as the play depicts it, eventually lead to Leontes' recovery of his lost daughter and the return of his wife. But they are the opposite of the hope expressed by his counselors that he will finally forgive himself and actively forge a new family. Instead what happens to him is the result of a series of circumstances over which he has no control, which take him and everyone else entirely by surprise.

The zaniness of these circumstances is epitomized by the petty thief Autolycus—"a snapper up of unconsidered trifles"—always on the lookout for his next victim. Halfway through the fourth act, he suddenly shows up, singing a song charged with the renewed sexual energy of spring:

> When daffodils begin to peer,
> With heigh, the doxy over the dale,
> Why, then comes in the sweet o' the year,
> For the red blood reigns in the winter's pale.

Bursting on the scene from nowhere, he serves as a sly image of the playwright himself as itinerant rogue, exuberant entertainer, cunning improviser, and thief. Like Autolycus, who declares that his "traffic is sheets," Shakespeare tears the sheets from *Pandosto* and repurposes them as a romance of the second chance, arbitrarily twisting the end in order to reunite the protagonist with his wife and daughter—and, not coincidentally, to give an unexpected, undeserved second chance to his own Lear and Othello.[35]

Because the jumbled events and motives in Bohemia—the elopement of the peasant girl and the prince, the alienation of the prince from his father, the nostalgic desire on the part of the Bohemian king's counselor to see his native Sicilia, the trickery of Autolycus, the desperate anxiety of the shepherd and his son, who reveal the tokens they happen to have saved for sixteen years—all turn out to lead to the climactic restoration, they assume the guise of occult instruments of a fated second chance. The play unembarrassedly has it both ways. It insists on contingency, random accident, and unexpected consequences. At the same time it traffics in mysterious destiny, the destiny hinted at darkly by Apollo's oracle: "the King shall live without an heir if that which is lost be not found." The realization of this destiny—and the oracle's "if" does not guarantee that it can be realized—does not come about because of any active role played by Leontes, such as he could have assumed, for example, by sending out searchers to scour the world for his lost daughter. Paulina, who argues against any comparable attempt by Leontes to seek another wife, suggests that there is no rational way to fulfill the oracle; the recovery of the abandoned Perdita is, she says, "monstrous to our human reason." But the daughter is recovered, and the tangle of seemingly random circumstances appears at least retrospectively to have been designed to lead to that result (as of course they were designed by Shakespeare).[36]

If in your own life you suffer a trauma, and, contrary to every rational expectation, you wind up getting a second chance, it will not, the play suggests, be because you have actively brought about the happy outcome. It will happen because of chains of circumstances beyond your control, because of changes invisible to you and outside the control of your will, because of the independent yet interlinked actions of a host of others, some of whom you already know (but with whom you may no longer be in direct contact), others whom you have never met and who know nothing about your regrets and longings. And if Paulina is any guide, it will happen because you have against all odds been patient, because you have learned to face your failings and to live with your trauma.

Just as Autolycus embodies randomness, Paulina—Leontes' guide through his years in the wasteland, constantly reminding him of what he has done, insisting that his first chance is gone forever, and urging him to wait patiently—embodies the play's intuition of a hidden design. (In the all-male performances of the early seventeenth century the same actor could have played both Autolycus and Paulina, so the figures of contingency and destiny might actually have been the same.) In the final scenes of the play Paulina emerges as a blend of magician and artist, creating illusions, manipulating expectations, arousing wonder, and fulfilling fantasies.

In the experience of a second chance, *The Winter's Tale* suggests, there is a peculiar air of make-believe, at once utterly convincing and at the same time indelibly tinged with fiction, wish-fulfillment, or witchcraft. "It is required," Paulina tells Leontes and the other onlookers, "You do awake your faith." Without the conviction that what seemed impossible can in fact happen, she insists, there is no going forward. Only then, ordering music to sound, does she turn to the statue of Hermione and say, "'Tis time; descend; be stone no more; approach. / Strike all that look upon with marvel." For the estranged husband and wife, the long period of suspended animation—Leontes having "shut up himself" and Hermione having found existence to be "no commodity"—is over. "Bequeath to death your numbness," she tells Hermione, for from death, "Dear life redeems you." Life has once again become "dear" to them; or, as Autolycus sings, "the red blood reigns in the winter's pale."[37]

Everything seems magically resolved. No longer hard, still, and cold as stone, Hermione descends from the pedestal. Leontes touches her hand and declares in astonishment, "O, she's warm!" As he routinely does when he wants to be absolutely sure that an action be represented, Shakespeare then adds lines that function as an inbuilt stage direction: "She embraces him," Polixenes says, and Camillo echoes, "She hangs about his neck." Leontes has got his second chance.[38]

And yet. Camillo immediately follows with what seems like a further piece of instruction—"If she pertain to life, let her speak too!"—but Hermione does not respond, nor does she provide what Polixenes too asks for: "Ay, and make it manifest where she has lived, / Or how stolen from the dead." Shakespeare leaves the questions unanswered. Yes, there is a second chance, but what that chance actually is and how the characters have reached it is not clear. Hermione's path is particularly obscure. Has she been brought back from the grave through some dark art, or was she in hiding, in a state of rage or numbness that has lasted sixteen years? The play signals both possibilities: on the one hand, Antigonus's lurid account, just before he dies, of seeing her shrieking ghost, on the other, the assurance that Paulina "hath privately twice or thrice a day ever since the death of Hermione" visited the secluded house in which she supposedly keeps the statue.[39]

It would have been easy enough for Shakespeare to provide definitive answers, but the play goes out of its way to highlight the incompleteness of the resolution it stages. Leontes has recovered his lost daughter, but he has not recognized her, and in the ways that matter most she now belongs to others—to the world of Bohemia, to her adoptive father, and to her betrothed. Having returned to warm life, Hermione puts her arms around Leontes' neck, but she says nothing to him, neither at the moment of the embrace nor for the remainder of the play. And Mamillius, the prince who was the reason those who "went on crutches ere he was born desire yet their life to see him a man" is dead. For the little boy there is no coming back to life, no second chance, any more than there is for Antigonus.[40]

Though an air of festive triumph reigns at the end of *The Winter's Tale*—one joy crowning another, as an awestruck bystander remarks—a strange sense remains that nothing is entirely settled or quite what it seems. True, the king has been united with his daughter, and his kingdom now, as the oracle had predicted, has an heir. But the heir is not his own son but the son of the man he had tried to poison, and the daughter is an unfamiliar young woman in whom he had just moments earlier expressed sexual interest. There is joy, but it is labile and unsettled and quickly turns to tears—as if the joy of the second chance were the gift of ordinary unhappiness, or "as if," one observer remarks, "joy were now become a loss."[41]

Through Paulina's witchlike power, Hermione has mysteriously come back from the dead. But in the midst of his experience of wonder, Leontes has already noticed something unsettling in the statue that Paulina has drawn back the curtain to show him: "Hermione was not so much wrinkled," he exclaims, "nothing / So aged as this seems." Though he is not at the moment looking into a mirror, his face also no doubt bears the evidence of how much he has aged. Shakespeare was always obsessed with the indelible marks of the passage of time; here the wrinkles are the signs of the years together as a couple that Leontes has lost—signs, that is, of his failed first chance. These marks are, as he puts it, "piercing to my soul." Time cannot be reversed.[42]

Whatever the second chance will mean for the reconstituted family, it will reflect what in the final moments of the play Leontes calls "this wide gap of time since first / We were dissevered." The initial surprise will fade, the faces will once again become familiar, and affairs may look as if they have picked up again where they left off. But even if, as here, it has the same cast of characters, the second chance is never the same as the first.[43]

A second chance gives Leontes the opportunity to recover his friend and his family, to recover his capacity to love, to re-create himself as the person he most wishes to be. It enables him once again to feel virtuous. But he cannot undo what he has done. Mamillius is gone forever; his daughter, now a young woman, is a complete stranger to him; his wife and friend will never forget his murderous rage. This is not a comedy, in which the pieces will miraculously be put together exactly as they were before they were scattered and seemingly lost. At the same time, Leontes is not simply turning the page and starting afresh, as his courtiers urged him to do, by marrying again and having a new family. The core group—wife, daughter, and friend—remains the same, despite all the changes that the years have wrought, and, just as important, Leontes remains Leontes. To be sure, the sixteen years have transformed him in crucial ways, but for Shakespeare a second chance involves continuity as well as difference. He is not a completely new man but rather a changed version of the old one. Hence he longs to repeat and revise the act that had initiated his insane jealousy. "Look upon my brother," he urges Hermione; "Both your pardons, / That e'er I put between your holy looks / My ill suspicion." By actively bringing about this repetition, he will demonstrate that he is a different person: the looks that had once driven him crazy—"How she holds up the neb, the bill, to him / And arms her with the boldness of a wife / To her allowing husband"—he will now deem "holy."[44]

But Hermione does not say a word either to Polixenes or to Leontes. She remains silent when she descends from the pedestal, when Camillo and Polixenes beg her to speak, and when Leontes directs her attention to Florizel, her prospective son-in-law. Her silence must have a meaning, but what exactly that is—and what it foretells for her future relationship with Leontes—is left unclear. She speaks once and once only, after she returns to life, her words directed to a single person in the crowded room. Calling on the gods to look down and bless her daughter, she bursts forth with a set of urgent questions and a telling explanation:

> Tell me, mine own,
> Where hast thou been preserved? Where lived? How
>   found

> Thy father's court? For thou shalt hear that I,
> Knowing by Paulina that the oracle
> Gave hope thou wast in being, have preserved
> Myself to see the issue.

The audience already knows the answer to the questions, but the fact that she preserved herself in the hope of seeing her daughter is something new. It suggests that for Hermione the second chance that matters is not reconciliation with Leontes and the resumption of her marriage but rather the recovery of the daughter torn from her just after her birth.[45]

We do not hear Perdita's response. "There's time enough for that," Paulina interrupts, "Lest they desire upon this push to trouble / Your joys with like relation."[46] The intervention is abrupt and rather obscure, but her words seem to mean that if Perdita begins to answer her mother's questions, others—Polixenes, Camillo, Florizel, and perhaps Leontes too—will feel the urge to tell their own stories of loss and recovery, their own versions of the chance that is theirs. Though much of the play has seemed to focus on Leontes—on his insane jealousy, his loss, his penitence, and his miraculous recovery of wife and daughter—for the other characters the significance of the story lies elsewhere: Hermione finds Perdita; Perdita, her identity revealed, is able to marry Florizel; Florizel now has an opportunity to reconcile himself with his father, Polixenes; Polixenes has an opportunity to prove himself a loving father; Camillo fulfills his desire to return to Sicilia; the shepherd and his son are pardoned and rewarded; Autolycus escapes the noose. Most of these stories are also second chances, independent of Leontes'. For much of the play the focus has been on Leontes' guilt, then on his grief, then on his restoration. For Shakespeare's audience that focus is the protagonist's privilege as a king and perhaps too as a man. But what if the story is not ultimately about his recovery? After all, the end of the play suggests, what you think of as your second chance may not be yours alone or, for that matter, may not count for others as particularly important.

Hermione tells Perdita that she was able to preserve herself "to see the issue." We are back to the question of why people, even when things become unbearable, stay alive. The term "issue" echoes constantly in *The Winter's Tale* (where it is used far more often than in any other play by Shakespeare). It means an outflowing or outcome; it refers to emergence or fluid movement in time; it implies that things do not remain static but rather develop, move, bend, twist, and burst forth. It refers to the result or the termination of a process—as when a minor character expresses her optimistic belief that Paulina's "undertaking cannot miss / A thriving issue." Above all, in this play it has, as in Hermione's speech, the sense that it retains today only in legal parlance: it signifies offspring.[47]

The word's paradoxical yoking of ending and beginning— of something coming to a close and something just coming into being—does not go unremarked; the play constantly works to bring together "things dying," as the old shepherd puts it, with "things newborn."[48] *The Winter's Tale* understands that the story of "issue" is not about birth alone but involves the whole of the life cycle. It understands too that from the perspective of "issue," the life cycle in question is not the passage of the individual from birth to death but the passage of reproductive capacity from one generation to the next. The play begins with the striking presence of the nine-months pregnant Hermione and ends with Hermione's return to existence at the point when the child that had been in her womb is now herself ready to breed.

The torch of the urgent desire to breed has been passed from one generation to the next. That is, in Paulina's phrase, "the law and process of great Nature," and the play's self-consciously archaic emblem of that process is the figure of Time turning his glass.[49] Everything depends upon the passage of time, upon trade-offs and transitions, upon the dance that leads the individual from birth to growth to sexual reproduction to senescence and to death, and that leads the whole natural world from one generative season to the next in an endless cycle of decay and renewal.

This cycle is the assurance of the world's second chance, an issue that does not extend to any of us as individuals. Perhaps even as he contemplated returning to Stratford to see if he could resume a relationship with his wife and daughters, Shakespeare reflected on this difference between the issue of an individual life and the issue of great creating nature. Or perhaps he put his faith in a different sense of *issue*—the outcome of a narrative, a story told so brilliantly it could be renewed in innumerably different ways until the end of time.

Though the play ends with a spectacular second chance, it suggests that such an outcome is a wish-fulfillment fantasy akin to the longing for a loved one to return from the dead or for a statue to come alive. As Shakespeare and his audience perfectly understood, after so disastrous a breakdown of trust, emotional renewal in real life, if it were to happen at all, was far more likely to take the form of a second marriage than an unexpected recovery of love in the first. But then Shakespeare and his audience lived in a world effectively without divorce. You could escape from a failed marriage and have a second chance if your spouse died—hardly a rare occurrence—but otherwise the only escape was to run away as far as possible, as perhaps Shakespeare himself had done when he left Stratford for London.

But if, as seems likely, when Shakespeare wrote *The Winter's Tale* he was contemplating a return to Stratford, then he needed to face the fact that the lawful wife, Anne Hathaway Shakespeare, was awaiting him there, along with his grown daughter Judith. From that point of view, a second marriage to a new wife would have been far more of a wish-fulfillment fantasy than the hope of renewing an existing marriage that had for many years been effectively held in suspension, as if his wife had been frozen in his mind, at least, into a statue. It is striking that when he revised Greene's story and changed the ending, Shakespeare did not—as he could easily have done—bring the little boy, Mamillius, back from the dead and restore to Leontes his only son along with Hermione. The boy is gone, and the only hope is to remake whatever life is possible with his wife and daughter.

The play represents this outcome as wildly implausible: "This news which is called true is so like an old tale that the verity of it is in strong suspicion." But it suggests at the same time that the hope for such an event is what makes existence bearable. It is the way in which life renews itself, akin to the return of the spring after a bleak winter, and hence it is at once astonishing, like an enchantment, and at the same time perfectly familiar and natural: "If this be magic," the awestruck Leontes declares, "let it be an art / Lawful as eating."[50]

5

Come Again
On Second Chances

The idea of the second chance is one of our more familiar self-cures for a certain kind of despair: the despair that comes from seeing ourselves as saboteurs of opportunity, as fundamentally self-destructive, distracted creatures, creatures whose hate is far stronger and stranger and more pleasurable than our love. The kind of despair, and desperation, we see so vividly in *The Winter's Tale*, generated at first in Paulina and the people who love and respect her, and eventually in Leontes himself because of what he has done and failed to do. Leontes' startlingly sudden and violent jealousy is like a terrorist attack, or the sudden eruption of a pandemic, setting off the drama of the play. And the idea of the second chance that Shakespeare uses the play to explore is, as always, an aftereffect of a catastrophe. What, if anything, can be gained—or more simply, made out of—devastating loss? This is the human, all-too-human question we are asking when we talk about second chances, a chance being at once an opportunity and something that might simply happen, beyond our doing. To talk about second chances is to wonder what Prince Hal's phrase "redeem-

ing time" could possibly mean. And indeed, to wonder what redemption might involve. How we might picture it.[1]

For Othello and Lear, unlike Leontes—though like Leontes, both Othello and Lear have to take the consequences of their
often apparently demonic jealousy and possessiveness—what
we have learned to call their tragedy is their determined and
intractable refusal of anything akin to a second chance (though
Lear, at least, does not refuse so much as miss the moment in
which he could have had a second chance—he was given multiple opportunities in the first act, but once he refused those he
received no further chances, missing the moment sometimes
being essential to the possibility of the second chance). That
second chance might have been born of these tragic heroes'
having doubts and remorse about what they have done to the
people they love and a desire to mend what was broken. The
second chance must present itself—by Hermione "miraculously"
coming back to life, say, or Perdita's return—and the person to
whom it is presented must then have the wherewithal and the
desire to see it as a second chance, and to take it. The second
chance implies, and takes for granted, that there was a first
chance, and that something about the first chance might have
misfired, or been spoiled or determinedly attacked. It is not, of
course, incidental that much of the literature we have come to
value is, one way or another, about second chances, about what
can and cannot be repaired, and about what that repair might
be (comedies are always comedies of recovery). The idea alone
of art as re-presentation, in whatever medium, has within it the
promise of a second time round, of a second look or a second
medium, that can be a second chance.

In Shakespeare's tragedies, what is represented is the so-
called tragic hero's incapacity for self-disillusionment, and so
for beneficial change; tragedies are always tragedies about the
violence of self-justification, the defending of an intractable po-

sition. What we see in tragedy is the worst-case scenario of the need to be right (what a life looks like as a protracted tantrum). The violence of the tragic heroes' jealousy, in order to be sustained, must be as unrelenting as their self-punishment, though it is never quite clear what is being protected or sustained by their righteous certainty, other than their righteous certainty itself. There must, after all, be good reasons why they behave as they do—reasons these tragedies want to make us wonder about and why their heroes can listen only to their accomplices and not to their critics; for there to be a second chance there has to be a critic—a revisionary critic—somewhere who can be listened to. They suffer from a lack of skepticism about themselves, as though a questioning of the self is an insulting of the self, or even a dismantling of the self (Leontes, like Lear and Othello, is furious whenever his actions are contested). They are in despair, one might say, about what their jealousy and their possessive individualism has led them to do; about their capacity for hatred; and about whether anyone can help them—their demand is for collusion, not for the voicing of alternatives. It is their despair, their helplessness, that has called up in them the faux potency of an irredeemable murderous rage. In this context the idea of the second chance seems, to the hero himself, like an absurd distraction. Whenever in these plays Lear or Othello or Leontes is asked to reconsider, he feels attacked, misunderstood, and betrayed.

It would be naive to say that jealousy, sexual jealousy, never brings out the best in us. But as these plays suggest—plays about the impossibility and the possibility of a second chance—we may need to think about what sexual jealousy brings out in us, and what that might reveal about ourselves as desiring creatures. And, indeed, about what self-doubt or its absence is being used to do by each character in the plays. If the tragedies are always studies in tyranny, whatever else they are, they are also

studies in the tyrant's relationship to himself, and how it super-
sedes or overrides his relations with others; this is what the
soliloquies are there to do—to make us concentrate on, by over-
hearing, the hero's relationship with himself. Tragedies are tragedies of sociability, of what people are doing to (and with) each
other and themselves when they agree and disagree. The always-
tyrannical tragic hero, one can say, enacts his doubt about
whether other people really exist, or really exist for him, whether
other people have anything to add, or anything he may need,
other than their willingness to obey him. It is, that is to say, the
tragic hero's relationship to help that is being dramatized. And
the second chance always depends on the help of others, and so
on a confidence in useful and enlivening exchange. The second
chance comes out of transforming collusion into collaboration,
turning self-sufficiency into a newfound kind of dependence.
Not unlike a conversion experience—to which it bears many
resemblances—the second chance often requires the dispelling
of many prior certainties, the revision of what had been taken
to be an essential self.

So in these plays we are left to wonder, What has to happen to someone, what must someone have done, to have no
doubt about inflicting pain on others—and, especially, on loved
others—and indeed, to have no doubt about inflicting pain
on himself? Time cannot be literally redeemed, or reversed;
we cannot go back to the time before the terrible things were
done, before we did the terrible things: at the time we meant to
do what we did, whatever the consequences may have been.
But the question—the question that makes the second chance
a possibility—is, What kind of conversations can our ineradi-
cable guilt make possible, or even inspire? Conversations both
with ourselves and with others; second chances are made with
words. Lear and Othello run out of conversations, and become
murderous; Leontes does not. And so *The Winter's Tale* inti-

mates that a tragedy—partly because it ends in death—might
also be an uncompleted action, and that this is what is tragic
about it. The tragic hero is someone who attacks his own development, who is continually waylaying his future, and the
futures of the people who care about him. We see the so-called
tragic hero at various points in the plays being given a second
chance (as though it were a temptation), and, unlike Leontes
(and Hermione and Perdita), being unable or unwilling to take
it. We see the possibility that the second chance, taken—or given,
which is, as we will see, an important distinction, if it is a distinction at all—might be among the very best things we do.
That morality itself begins with the idea of the second chance.
Or, to put it differently, that the idea of the second chance is a
way of imagining ourselves at our best.

In the second chance we get, if there is one, there is always, then, the chance of finally realizing our preferred version
of ourselves (if you want to picture your ambition for yourself
you have to imagine what you would do if you got a second
chance). The as-yet unlived life that is our second chance carries what we presume to be our potential. Our second chance
must be, at least in prospect, better than our first. It is an opportunity for something to come to life, or to come to more life. It
is an opportunity to formulate what we might want for ourselves,
and for the other people in our lives. The second chance may
begin as a wish—or even as a utopian fantasy—but everything
depends upon how it is worked out, and on how it works out.

In the Christian tradition, to be born in a state of original sin
might offer someone the second chance of being saved, whether
or not redemption is assumed to be a gift (of God) or an achievement, whether or not it is within a person's grasp. Indeed, it is
the promise of religions that they offer the follower these possibilities for, these means of, dramatic transformation. Religions

are committed to self-improvement and so to the assumption that the individual is in need of such improvement, and capable of it, and thus always in need of the second chance that the whole notion of self-improvement offers. (Self-improvement is not available, of course, to Calvin's already damned.) In a religious context, it is effectively the second chance that makes the life worth living, the allure of being better, even if the criteria for what it is to be better are always up for grabs, there to be argued about. The first chance, the life one is born into, is there for the second chance (of being better) to be fulfilled. Believers, though, tend not to refer to the state of original sin as their first chance, any more than children refer to their parents as their first chance, or than people's first experience of learning to walk, or talk, or read, or have sex is described as a first chance, though each of these is. And so, by the same token, we can wonder how second chances may be affected by taking into consideration first chances.

But in a world without Providential design, chances, unanticipated opportunities, tend to be for atheists. To believe that your life is made of, or made out of, chances means not to think of contingency as something like a god. In a more secular context—in which the good life and a person's potential to live a good life have been radically redescribed (no redemption, no afterlife, no fixed faiths, no destiny or fate)—the first chance rarely feels like a first chance, nor is it described as such. Indeed it is only when something seems to be a second chance that we can recognize what, in our secular lives, our first chances might have been, or been taken to be, or what we might have wanted them to have been. As *The Winter's Tale* suggests, it is only when a second chance seems to offer itself that we can begin to see what our first chances actually were—chances not taken or recognized, or chances not wanted. Leontes did not think of his earlier, almost idyllic relationships with his boyhood friend Polixenes and his wife, Hermione, as in any sense first chances for anything. Those relationships were just the good fortune that was his life. But once he set about destroying them in a fit of demonic jealousy—once these two people were lost from his life—he began to see them, to value them (and himself) in a quite different way.

The second chance reveals the first chance to be an opportunity missed, or sabotaged, or simply unacknowledged, and suggests that a life—like a play—is the kind of thing that can be rehearsed. Like an uncompleted action the first chance seems to be something aborted, or preempted (recognition is often prompted or revised by loss). And by the same token, any sense of continuity in a life—that is to say, any narrative of a life that is a narrative of intelligible, as opposed to random, incoherent change—depends in some way or another on the possibility of the second chance, as the repetition of something that can be reworked (when Hermione and Perdita return, Leontes can love them again in a different way, a way that must acknowledge what has happened between them over time). People are always older when they get a second chance. The second chance is never the same as the first, as we have said, partly because it is the product, so to speak, of what we have come to realize was our first chance for something or other (Leontes' second chance of loving Polixenes, Hermione, and his daughter is drastically different from his first chance but depends upon it). If something is experienced as a second chance it reassures us that repetition is not merely and solely more of the same, or simply mechanistic, or arbitrary and meaningless, for it is only repetition that makes improvisation possible; we can be the authors of our own lives and not merely the victims, or the actors, of them.

The idea of the second chance, then, restores or prompts a sense of agency, of our being able to make our own lives as well as being made by them. The second chance, that is to say, for better and for worse, helps us to believe in mastery, among other things; and so-called mastery, for better and for worse, can make us believe that our lives are our own. If we did not think of life as offering us second chances, of allowing us opportunities to revise or repair or improve, our lives would seem merely disjointedly episodic and gratuitous; and we ourselves would be creatures without choice or potential or judgment or direction. If we no longer believed in recovery—in punishment or redemption or guilt—we would not know what to do with ourselves, would not know what we wanted to become, what we wanted to do next, or what we were looking forward to. We would not know how to proceed. If we were condemned by our first mistake we would never learn anything, since we can often begin only if we know that we will be able to try again (though we do perhaps need to bear in mind that in Augustinian Christianity we are condemned by our first mistake). Without the whole notion of the second chance we would have to re-imagine hope, and progress, and pleasure. We would have to reimagine what it would be to be, or to have, a character. We may not think of the play we see as a second chance for the rehearsals, or the performed music as a second chance for the practice that has made it possible; but once we do, both preparation and performance look different. More open to innovation, say, or re-creation, or reworking.

We may not always take it for granted that we will get a second chance, and there are many occasions when we will not. But that we may have a second chance will make all the difference to what we do and how we do it. Tragic heroes believe (wrongly) they have been betrayed by people they love and need, that they have been humiliatingly naive and inattentive, and that that betrayal is irreparable. And they believe above all in their belief; they are adept at radically narrowing their own minds, and then being spellbound by their own restricted thoughts: tragedies are dramas about what it is to believe something, and to believe in someone, about what belief should or should not entail. Madness, the psychoanalyst D. W. Winnicott famously remarked, is the need to be believed. Shakespeare's tragic heroes believe—need to believe—that in love there can be no second chances. That the only solution to betrayal is revenge, usually murder, which will turn trauma into triumph. That disillusionment with the women they love is terminal, and leads only to death or murder. It is assumed that they cannot be, in the best sense, re-illusioned, re-enchanted, and reassured again by the women they loved. What we have learned to call pride, or narcissism, or arrogance could be redescribed as simply a determined hatred of the second chance. (There are, though, some interesting exceptions—or complications—to these claims, in, for example *Romeo and Juliet* and *Coriolanus*.) Winnicott, as we shall see, went on to describe a developmental theory in which to love is, by definition, to experience and believe in the second chance. In his version of real love, so to speak, it is always and only, and can only be, a second chance; and so real love—or at least real exchange between people, real relationship, in his sense of real—can only come out of a gradual disillusionment with oneself and the other person; it is, that is to say, the product of a supposed betrayal. The child, says Winnicott, betrays his or her parents (and endangers him- or herself) by hating them, the people the child loves and needs, and thus the child's ambivalence, the child's love and hate, are a threat to his or her well-being. The parent betrays the child by becoming a real person to the child and not merely a wished-for person, not a figure of fantasy, exclusively meeting the child's needs. (Parents are inevitably ambivalent about their own children: *Oedipus*, after all, is also a story about the murderous wishes of parents in relation to their children.) In Winnicott's story of child development, the inevitability of things going wrong initially between parents and children—and eventually between adults in their various relationships—is taken for granted, everything depending on how things are repaired and whether they can be repaired. *Reparation* is another word for the second chance. And the second chance is another way of talking about development.

In the tragedies we have been talking about there is despair about the possibility of repair, acknowledgment, one might say, of the irreparable; of the second chance that is a making of amends, a making up in the fullest sense. For Winnicott love is an endless and ongoing process of illusionment and disillusionment—a falling in and out of love that is the definition of love, of love as something that develops and deepens, a repeated and cumulative (and precarious) cycle of first and of second chances that can, at any moment, be sabotaged. As we shall see, for Winnicott, illusionment (falling in love) without the subsequent disillusionment (disappointment) is disengaged and futile and enraged; and the disillusionment that does not lead to a future re-illusionment (a re-enchantment), forecloses development. Shakespeare's late plays, one could say, are about ways of surviving disillusionment.

But before we look at Winnicott's children we must look at Freud's, who are also determined to get a second chance. After all, what is the so-called Oedipus complex, what is the relinquishing of incestuous desire and leaving home but a second chance at love, a second chance at love that is the first real chance at sex? Adult love and sexuality are described by Freud as inspired and made both possible and viable by the inevitable defeats and failures of the child's love and desire for the parents. By refusing and setting limits to their children's desire for them—and their desires, such as they are, for their children—the parents become the guardians of their children's future erotic lives. (Lear's catastrophic love test is the dramatic sabotaging of this protective role.) Children can become adults, in Freud's view, only if their love as adults is a second chance (only if you fail to marry your mother will you be able to marry someone else). Adults can continue growing only if they can go on forever using their childhood experience as material for the second chance that is adulthood.

Freud's children do not initially believe in love as a second chance—they would in part prefer to stick to their love for their parents, at least until adolescence—but they will need to if they are to grow up in the Freudian way. And as a consequence, perhaps, second chances are everywhere in Freud's work. Indeed, if, as we suggest, Shakespeare did design *The Winter's Tale* as, among other things, a template for understanding the challenge and the possibility of a second chance, then we can also say, more sweepingly, that much of Freud's work— and the work of some of his followers, who have wanted to give psychoanalysis a second chance—frames and formulates our abiding preoccupation with second chances. Freud is our great modern champion and our exemplary theorist of the second chance. His own second chances included becoming a successful doctor from unpromising Eastern European Jewish origins in anti-Semitic Vienna, and then inventing psychoanalysis after the unwanted rigors of training to be a medical doctor. Whether he is writing about the notorious Oedipus complex or mourning as the precondition for a new relationship or narcissism as an attack on the need for, on the wish for, a second chance; or about what he calls "deferred action," in which experiences—and particularly traumatic events—become meaningful (or even visible) only when they have been revised or redescribed after they happen; or about the so-called return of the repressed, in which you can only recognize something about yourself when it returns, when it repeats itself, after first being denied, he is always writing and rewriting about revision and repair. The idea, the necessity, of the second chance is the heart of the matter for Freud. As if to say, modern people can only understand their lives in the light of second chances (and third and fourth chances, though these are phrases we do not use, as though the second chance were the one we needed to keep in mind). As if without the possibility of the second chance there is no life worth living.

All these Freudian accounts want to convince us that there is a sense in which there are no first chances—no developmental first chances perceived as such at the time—only second chances, taken or not; that experiences can only become real—can only become experiences in any meaningful or useful sense—the second time round; that prospect comes out of retrospect (it is the dream, in Freud's view, that makes the dream day—the day before the night's dream—meaningful). And what makes the second time round a second chance, at least for Freud, is the possibility of putting something into words—of rediscovering our experience through redescribing it in ways that make a future, in ways that make us think, or make it possible for us to think—which the first time round was impossible or unwanted. Traumas, psychoanalysis would suggest, are the experiences we are unable to have; they have to be turned into experiences through the second chance of being able to remember and re-create them by speaking about them to an attentive listener. Without the second chance the first chance is a haunting persecution; an experience that preempts future experience (which is one definition of a trauma). Certainly, for Freud, adulthood is the second chance of childhood, the redeeming of the desires and traumas of childhood to make them generative, to give them a future.

But childhood, we could say, is one second chance after

another—a continual experiment in living—but without the adult sense of what it is to have a second chance. Or, to put it slightly differently, to acquire the sense of there being second chances, which the tragic hero is unable to do—to learn the phrase and enjoy the prospect—is a developmental achievement. It is a new picture of what the future could be. And in part because it gives us a sense of what the past might be for. So to describe Shakespeare as constructing a "wild experiment"— what if, say, Othello were granted a second chance in the marriage he had wrecked—is to describe what might happen when the whole notion of the second chance is recycled, brought into play. As if to say, pragmatically, Where in our lives might the idea of the second chance work, or be useful, or interesting? Shakespearean tragedy and modern psychoanalytic child development, among many other things, show us what second chances can be used for.

Children, for example, do not assume when they are growing up that they will get a second chance at being parented. But they are nevertheless often adept at finding mother and father figures that significantly extend the range of their experience. And they do not, of course, think of these people as a second chance, or indeed of their parents as their first chance; their parents, their family, are simply their life. And yet, as Freud suggested in his essay appropriately titled "Family Romances"— implying that the family is itself a romance of various kinds, and hopefully the first of many—a point comes when it begins to dawn on the child that her or his parents cannot possibly be the true parents. They are too dull to be the parents of someone as extraordinary as the child. They are clearly inadequate for the task of bringing up such a child. And it is, Freud says, reactive to "the most intense impulses of sexual rivalry" with parents and siblings that the child begins to construct an alternative reality (Shakespeare's tragic heroes, we should remember, are suffering

from just these intense impulses). "A feeling of being slighted,"
Freud writes, "constitutes the subject matter of such provoca-
tions." After being slighted,

> the child's imagination becomes engaged in the task
> of getting free from the parents of whom he now
> has a low opinion and of replacing them by others,
> who, as a rule, are of higher social standing. He will
> make use in this connection of any opportune co-
> incidences from his actual experience, such as his
> becoming acquainted with the Lord of the Manor
> or some landed proprietor if he lives in the country,
> or with some member of the aristocracy if he lives
> in town.[2]

It is disappointment, in this case with the parents, that makes
the child imaginative. And what the child imagines is, from our
point of view, a second chance of being parented but is, from
the child's point of view, the first chance of being parented that
the child was naturally entitled to but missed out on. The child
though, like all believers in the second chance, is trying to correct something, to put something to rights: second chances are
as much about justice as they are about love. The child, that is
to say, in this state of mind does not believe in, cannot contemplate, absolute and irreversible loss; cannot bear the prospect
of relinquishing the parent she or he is entitled to, and the potential the child can realize in her- or himself. Like all believers
in the second chance, these children do not, or cannot, bear to
believe in irredeemable loss. Indeed, it is precisely experiencing the possibility of such loss that makes them "creative," that
inspires the second chance. They see loss as opportunity, they
see deprivation as prompting recovery, they see betrayal as
inspiring self-doubt; they see doubt as the precondition for the

second chance. Adam and Eve felt expelled and exiled and above all punished when they left the Garden of Eden. Second-chancers find ways of being or becoming enlivened, invigorated, reborn through their sufferings and misdemeanors, and punishments. ("If you lose all hope, you can always find it again," says the hero of Richard Ford's *The Sportswriter,* a remarkable contemporary celebration of second chances.)[3] It is only in the aftermath of catastrophe that their lives can begin. Freud—who had been himself unusually adept at finding more inspiring parents than his own in his scientist teachers and what he called the "great imaginative writers"—like the children he describes in "Family Romances," wants to make loss and deprivation work for him. What he has lost or been deprived of is the clue to what he might want, the chance missed a clue to the chance wanted. Not believing in second chances is the defeatedness of the resentful and the unimaginative. If hearts are made to be broken, as Oscar Wilde remarked, then first chances are made to become second ones.[4]

As with Shakespeare's Leontes, it is from what might be called now a narcissistic wound—a mortifying threat to his preferred picture of himself—that Leontes is given a second chance; second chances, as we say, often depend on something happening out of sight, something uncalculated. But Freud's children devise second chances, new parents, and therefore new developmental possibilities. This, one could say, is the second chance as also revenge, the violent putting to rights of what is felt to be a radical injustice. And it is indeed one of the many interesting things about the idea of the second chance that one cannot always distinguish the revenge from the reparation: revenge is more often ersatz reparation, or a despair about its real possibility. But the ingenious imagination of these Freudian children suggests a wish or a will—or even a determination— for the second chance, as though one's psychic survival or emotional development depends on an absolute commitment to the second chance. Freud's account of the Oedipus complex implies, as I say, some innate or "natural" commitment to what we have come to call the second chance; it implies that a belief in second chances is a precondition for development, or what we may prefer to call, less biologically, a good life. What Shakespeare did not show us was a tragic hero having a change of heart (perhaps by definition a tragic hero is someone incapable of a change of heart; tragedies show us what this looks like). Leontes, one could say, was lucky enough to get a second chance and so avoid a wholly tragic fate; he loses a son as the consequence of his actions, but recovers, in a sense, a wife and daughter. So we should distinguish—and Freud helps us do this—between the second chance taken, and the second chance given. The tragic hero cannot recognize a second chance, or recognize a second chance as being of value, and so cannot take one; Leontes was lucky enough to be given one, and to be able to take it. And what is instructive about *The Winter's Tale* is that it invites us to wonder both what a second chance is—how it can come about, what might make it happen—and what might predispose someone to take it, as Leontes does. Shakespeare shows us the far-reaching and unfolding tragedy of Leontes and what he has done, and, most crucially, what has to happen for the tragedy to be (partly) averted.

Winnicott, however, following on from Freud, gives us a developmental theory that combines both these versions—the giving of the second chance, and the taking of the second chance—in a way that makes them inextricable. For Winnicott the child has to be given a second chance (by the mother) in order to take one (as his or her own desire). And the child's desire, in Winnicott's account, is to satisfy his or her appetite and to have a relationship with a real mother, a mother conceived of as an independent person not under remote control by the child, all in the service of the child's own optimal development. But a child can be given a second chance only if that child has, or has been given, the wherewithal to take it; and, of course, the child can take it only if it is there to be taken. And the second chance that the Winnicottian child is seeking is a relationship with the real parents after having had only, to begin with, a relationship with the parents in fantasy. Once again, the child's first quest for the second chance is a quest for more satisfying parents. The second chance is always a chance for a greater satisfaction, and for the greater satisfaction that comes out of a more realistic intimacy. Winnicott's version of the good life is one in which there is a continual giving and taking of second chances between people.

In the rather strange and sometimes literal language of psychoanalysis, Winnicott imagines the baby, in a state of hunger, fantasizing the gratifying breast; and if the mother is sufficiently attentive—is, what he calls, a "good-enough" mother—she will keenly give the baby the breast when he or she is hungry (her desire will be to satisfy the baby). And because there is not much delay between the child's hunger and the arrival of the breast, the child assumes, in Winnicott's view, that he or she has the mother under omnipotent control. To want is to have, for the baby. This is the child's first experience of appetite, if all goes well; we might call it the child's first chance (at survival, at hunger, at satisfaction, at omnipotence, at development), but for the child this is simply what life is. In a life of omnipotence there is no such thing as a second chance, for there is no need for one. (God, by definition, does not have, and could not possibly need, second chances.) In this state of what Winnicott calls "illusion" the child is his or her own guarantee; the child's illusion is that he or she has total control over what he or she needs, that it effectively comes from the child, and exactly when he or she wants it. "To the observer," Winnicott writes in *Playing and Reality*,

> the child perceives what the mother actually presents [her breast], but this is not the whole truth. The infant perceives the breast only in so far as a breast could be created just there and then. There is no interchange between the mother and infant. Psychologically the infant takes from a breast that is part of the infant, and the mother gives milk to an infant that is part of herself. . . . [T]he idea of interchange is based on an illusion in the psychologist.[5]

In this picture of the baby's first chance at appetite and development, there is from the child's—and in a different sense, the mother's—point of view no exchange. From the baby's point of view there is no one to exchange anything with. In the child's first relationship with so-called external reality, there is no separate reality, and it is not external.

Disillusionment—the apprehension of external reality—comes a bit later, when it begins to dawn on the child that the mother is separate and independent of the child; indeed, she sometimes seems to be a law unto herself (i.e., not under the child's omnipotent control). And this is when the trouble and the real development start, when frustration and hatred enter the picture, and when, by the same token, the second chance can appear (before the frustration, very little ambivalence was called up to disturb the child). The second chance for the child (and for the adult the child will become) is the possibility of living happily enough—wanting to live—knowing that the child does not control the person he or she needs. Of living in relation to reality, a reality that is beyond the child's control. The drawback of the second chance is that the child has to learn to bear frustration; the advantage of this second chance is that the child no longer needs to depend on a figure of his or her own fantasy (the child can avoid the strain of self-sufficiency). The child can now discover that there is so much more to the mother, to him- or herself, and to their relationship with each other than the literal gratifying of instinctual need, though the gratifying of instinctual need is at the heart of the matter; everything starts from there and returns to there. The second chance means being able, at best, to enjoy dependence on someone who does not belong to you; and because that person is not your invention—is external to you—there is more to the person than you can imagine. This, of course, cuts both ways.

What I am calling the second chance here—the second chance for love and appetite and growth, for a (nourishing) relationship to reality—depends for Winnicott on the mother being sufficiently reliable and able to bear, without too much retaliation, the infant's frustrated rage—the child's hatred of the mother for frustrating him or her. And it depends on the child being enabled by the mother, as far as is possible, to bear this frustration and hatred by her not being too tantalizing and unpredictable. As Winnicott writes, rather horrifyingly, in *Playing and Reality,*

> The feeling of the mother's existence lasts x minutes. If the mother is away more than x minutes, then the imago [image of the mother in the child's mind] fades.... The baby is distressed, but this distress is soon *mended* because the mother returns in $x+y$ minutes. In $x+y$ minutes the baby has not become altered. But in $x+y+z$ minutes the baby has become *traumatized.* In $x+y+z$ minutes the mother's return does not mend the baby's altered state. Trauma implies that the baby has experienced a break in

life's continuity. . . . Madness here simply means a
break-up of whatever may exist at the time of a *personal continuity* of existence. After "recovery" from
$x+y+z$ deprivation a baby has to start again permanently deprived of the root which could provide
continuity with the personal beginning.[6]

If the child waits for the mother, and she returns within a bearable space of time, and this happens again and again, the child
develops a cumulative belief in the second chance—the mother
leaves, but she returns (the mother, at her best, who keeps returning, is our first experience of the second chance). There is
always a second chance; there is no absolute and irredeemable
loss. If the mother returns after what Winnicott calls "$x+y+z$
minutes," she to all intents and purposes dies for the child; the
child then has to mobilize drastic defenses to protect him- or
herself—to insulate him- or herself from, to inure him- or herself to this experience; and the child learns to live, traumatized,
without the recurring assurance of the second chance (the image
is of profound rupture and uprooting). We will only believe in
the second chance if we have not had to wait too long, as children, for what we need, for what (who) our life depends upon.
We will only truly believe in the second chance if we can let
ourselves wait without needing to control, or believe we are
controlling or have to control, the person we are waiting for and
need. When we wait too long for those we are looking forward
to seeing we cannot enjoy them when they arrive; we cannot
easily give them, and ourselves, a second chance: the grudge is
the refuge from the second chance. Only the person we cannot
control—the person beyond our omnipotence—is sufficiently
real for us to be able to have a real exchange, a real relationship
with. We can create a meal in our imagination, but it will not
nourish us. In Winnicott's terms the first meal is the one we

imagine; only its second chance as a real meal will feed us. Reality is the second chance for fantasy. Fantasy without reality is maddening; reality without fantasy is unappetizing.

The child has to be given the second chance by the mother's continued reliability—by her continual attentive return—and has to be able to take that chance based on his or her experience of this continued reliability. If the child has had to wait $x+y+z$ minutes he or she will have to live without—and won't be able to afford to recognize—the second chance. Because what looks like the second chance brings with it the second chance of repeating the initial trauma. The traumatized person, in this account, has to spend his or her life guarding against the recognition and the temptation of the second chance.

To redescribe tragedy as trauma, as the deferred consequence of traumatic rupture from the mother, may be more or less illuminating. But we must be wary now of mapping culturally and historically distinct languages onto each other. What may be of significance is what can be said, both about Shakespearean tragedy—and the avoidance of tragedy that is *The Winter's Tale*—and about psychoanalytic child development in light of the idea of the second chance. And by the same token, what they can both tell us about the need and the terror of the only other chance that is named and numbered. In any guide to the experience of the second chance we need to know, at its most minimal, what is at stake in the avoidance, or the refusal, or the denial of the second chance. And what may be lost when the second chance is lost.

6

Remembering Second Chances
Freud and Proust

A second chance is always an act of remembering, whatever else it is. When we talk about second chances we are talking, by definition, about the workings of memory; the recovery in memory of what may seem now, at least in retrospect, to have been a first chance. In recognizing what we take to be a second chance we are remembering something, even if we are not quite certain what it was. So one of the things we are doing in making or taking or being given a second chance is reconstructing the past. Reconstructing it, but also seeing it in a particular way. Seeing it, for example, as a series of opportunities, more or less taken. Given a second chance to do something, we may realize, say, on looking back that an experience that disappointed us was, in fact, a missed opportunity, one that can now be, in some way, repaired. That what felt inevitable then may have been, in some sense, chosen, and that we can choose again.

So the whole idea of second chances makes us, unavoidably, the historians, the interpreters, the readers of our own pasts. The second chance always reveals, as I say, what our first chances were, whether we realized it at the time or not. And once something seems like a second chance it is as if there were a pattern, a logic, a coherence to our lives. As if our lives could be a kind of narrative—a story of repetitions and recurrences— rather than a haphazard and random series of episodes. If repetition with improvisation is the preferred story of our lives, then second chances become an imperative part of a good life. The prospect of a second chance, a mixture perhaps of luck and judgment, keeps us hopeful. In a life that is not merely episodic— or a life simply devoted to self-improvement—the second chance is what we have to look forward to.

But being given a second chance to take an exam, or after breaking a promise, or instead of being punished is clearly quite different from thinking of a new relationship as some kind of second chance. Second chances clearly come in many forms, and it is interesting in itself to note the areas of our lives in which it turns up as a good way of describing something. It is not always obvious, for example, what kind of second chance a second marriage is—what Stanley Cavell refers to, apropos of the Hollywood films of a certain period, as the comedy of remarriage, reminding us of the comic potential of the second chance.[1] How much depends upon its difference from the first, and how much does this difference make it possible to do familiar, habitual, supposedly neurotic things differently? If who I am is a function, a consequence of my relationships, then a new relationship can be a new start (for me). If who I am is a consequence of my history, I am likely to bring the tyrannies and dramas from my past into my remarriage. And even if we acknowledge that both things may be true, we need to ask, What is it about ourselves, what is it about our lives, that can realistically get, or be given, a second chance? When is "a second chance" a useful way of describing a remarriage? Because what we want a second chance to do for us, when we have recognized it, is not always entirely clear, informed as it is by a great deal of wishfulness, as well as by what we have heard concerning second chances. What we want from a second chance is going to be different from what we get from a second chance. And unsurprisingly, it is precisely these doubts and hopes and questions and misgivings that haunt the work of the two modern masters, so to speak, of the second chance, Freud and Proust. The second chance as a particular and formative kind of opportunity effectively organizes their writing, as do fundamental questions about memory. Freud and Proust are fascinated both by what it is that makes a chance feel "second"—that makes it feel like a crucial repetition—and by what about it can be described as a chance; the word itself suggests something gratuitous and unarranged, but also usable and there for our benefit.

For Freud, as we shall see, all desiring is a form of remembering; it always links us to our earliest desiring and to our losses. The second chance for the young desiring oedipal child comes at puberty, and so is fraught with the largely unconscious history of the pleasures and calamities of childhood (psychoanalysis, at its most lugubrious, speaks of the "cumulative trauma" of childhood).[2] And then psychoanalytic treatment—as what Freud calls "an after-education"—provides the adult with another second chance, an opportunity to resolve, insofar as it is possible, the conflicts and perplexities of the desiring adult. And what Freud gradually discovered was how ambivalent people were about their second chances: adolescence was often tumultuous, and patients tended to resist psychoanalytic treatment as much as, if not more than, they welcomed it. People were extremely ambivalent, Freud realized, about second chances.

For Proust, in *In Search of Lost Time,* in which the lost time of the past is often conceived of as a series of first chances more or less realized—and often realized only through being remembered—the question is always whether our experiences in the past will be given the second chance of being remembered. For Proust remembering itself is a second chance, wherever it happens to lead; second chances are not obviously instrumental or available for any kind of known purpose. Proust, who is not a pragmatist, is preoccupied with how the past turns up, how it just occurs to us for no apparent reason, whether or not it becomes available for use, for contemplation and inspiration and recovery, for clues about the desired, or desirable, future. And where Freud sees patients often attacking the possibility or the actuality of the second chance by forgetting and distorting their memory of the past—wanting to stay stuck with their childhood desires and conflicts, and solutions—Proust sees the second chance provided by memory as almost entirely gratuitous, beyond our control, and not always wanted. (Both Freud and Proust are excessively mindful, in different ways, of memory as trauma.) Much of our past is lost irretrievably, Proust shows us, because nothing has triggered our memory of it. And whether or not our memories of the past are called up is entirely dependent on chance. We miss a myriad of second chances in our lives because of unprompted memory. We happen to hear something, or smell something—or more famously in Proust taste something, a madeleine—and the past returns as if by magic, given the second chance of being remembered. But so much vanishes without trace. And we cannot, in Proust's view, engineer significant remembering, whereas Freud believes that we can at least create the conditions for it in psychoanalytic treatment. Indeed, Freud wants us to actively seek out and articulate the second chances that memory can provide. Proust simply wants us to get lucky. We find and make our second chances or they just happen to happen to us.

Psychoanalysis is the quest romance that seeks out second chances. Proust wants them but knows they cannot be looked for or actively sought. (In Proust it is not always clear whether it is we or the past that is given a second chance by being remembered.) It is part of Freud's therapeutic intent that we should get the benefit of our past; and this can only be done through the second chances of remembering. And Freud wants the patient to, as it were, try and remember through free association. Freud believes he has a method for the remembering that Proust believes to be exempt from method and intention. In Proust the second chances given by memory come more as grace, whereas psychoanalytic treatment is more like work (clearly, talking about second chances never floats free of the language of its religious precursors). But either way, some notion of the second chance and of how much hangs on it, and of the second chance being something to do with memory, is, as we shall see, at the heart of the matter for both these modern writers.

As Freud and Proust in their different ways make clear, the idea of the second chance privileges experience over innocence, linking comprehension and competence into a reassuring story, a story in which the past—which may inform everything but determine nothing—is our greatest resource. A story in which there can be benign gods, benign fates, benign natural laws, a world of faith and hope and renewal, and in which we have some freedom to live the lives we want. Lives in which we can have second chances are lives in which there are redeemable opportunities. Through some kind of knowledge or understanding, or access, the past—and our desires and ambitions—can be recovered, or reworked, or revised to our advantage. To have or make or take a second chance, in other words, we must be able to learn from experience; we must be able to have memories and to find ways of valuing and in some way using them to make a future. And clearly a capacity to learn from experience is one of our most cherished and compelling progress myths; and it is, of course, the subject of most plays and novels, and indeed of psychoanalysis itself. It promises us that what comes after, what comes later, can or should be better than what we start from; that there are selves we can be that are better than the selves we are; that origins are not what matter but what we make of them; that we are able to do something with our innocence, or our naïveté, or our immaturity, or indeed our inexperience that turns it into a resource. That we can become better at becoming ourselves and can recognize what kind of better it is better to be. To identify an opportunity as a second chance is to be, in a certain way, very knowing.

Second chances, that is to say, make us wonder what it might be to learn from experience. "Most people," the psychologist William James is reputed to have said, "never run far enough on their first wind to find out they've got a second." There is then, though it sounds counterintuitive, a resistance to second chances—to a life being revised for the better—that Freud, and his followers, became preoccupied with, if not actually obsessed by. (Once you identify self-destructiveness you can see it everywhere; once resistance is recognized, it seems to inform virtually everything we do.) Freud began to realize, the farther into the practice of psychoanalytic treatment he got, that his so-called patients wanted to change by remaining the same. That patients who claimed to want help often recruited the analyst to help them not to change. That patients could be unconsciously phobic about there being second chances at all, and so would mobilize what Freud referred to as "a negative therapeutic reaction."[3] A patient's desire for the treatment and its success would be trumped by his or her resistance to being cured. And he or she would work against the doctor while appearing to cooperate. What people did unconsciously was often at odds, Freud noticed early in his work, with what they said they were doing. It took him some time, perhaps understandably, to apply this to people who wanted the second chance of being helped. Freud had to come to terms with the fact that unconsciously people often did *not* want to be helped. Their first chances had been more than enough. They wanted to stick with them. Indeed their lives seemed to be simply the unfolding of formative first chances. People, as we say, never really change.

James's example is vivid because it brings in the whole notion of staying power, of the persistence required to get to the second wind. That a certain kind of determination, a certain kind of work, may be required to get to the second chance that is a second wind (Freud would call this the overcoming of resistances, as though resistance were like stage fright). Because what Freud kept finding was that however optimistic and ambitious to change his patients were—however eager to give themselves the second chance of symptom-cure, or of resolving a developmental arrest—unconsciously they were radically resistant to any opportunity provided. When it came to the progress myths of their culture—economic, scientific, artistic—Freud's psychoanalytic patients provided a strange and haunting exposé. Underlying the fervent belief in progress—in a better life, in a better world—was not merely a despair about the capacity for change but a refusal of the desire for change. It was not that Freud's patients had no belief in second chances—why else would they see a psychoanalyst?—it was that they did not really want them. Freud was increasingly to devote his work to explaining his patients' aversion to the second chance that change always is.

The analyst starts explaining, the psychoanalyst Jacques Lacan once suggested, when he or she is frightened of his or her curiosity. As we shall see, Freud was as, if not more, daunted by his patients' attack on their development—by their hatred of the second chances that psychobiological development continually provides—as he was by their sexuality or their violence. He discovered how passionately people wanted to believe that they were stuck; it was precisely second chances that they dreaded. They preferred their suffering to their opportunities (no masochist really wants a second chance). Every child was ambivalent about adulthood as an object of desire. Freud discovered, in other words, that to be curious about second chances and the avoidance of second chances led him to some distasteful truths about so-called human nature. Not least of which was that many modern people wanted less rather than more life, that anesthesia and inertia and unconsciousness were for many modern people their objects of desire. That people would go to great and violent lengths to sabotage themselves. Like the Shakespearean tragic heroes we have discussed—though with far fewer good lines—many of Freud's patients seemed to be intent on spoiling, on waylaying the possibility of second chances.

When Freud is writing about resistances and defenses he is writing about people's refusal of a second chance, their need to fix and formulate themselves, their need to keep recovery at bay (recovery, in which something is recovered—a desire, a memory, a thought—with a view to it being given a second chance). When Freud wrote in his dismayed late paper "Analysis Terminable and Interminable," "The defensive mechanisms directed against former danger recur in the treatment as resistances against recovery. It follows from this that the ego treats recovery itself as a new danger," he was reconstructing the drama by which patients will not let themselves remember, will not let themselves get to a second wind.[4] There was originally a danger, probably in childhood, Freud proposes—a dangerous wish, a dangerous feeling, a dangerous situation in the outside world—which was responded to, defended against, almost as a reflex, and which then became a bad but reassuring habit; and this habit is called a symptom. Every time I miss someone I get a headache; every time there is an argument I feel faint; and these symptoms function as self-cures, as my repertoire of solutions to what I experience as unbearably disturbing predicaments. And

the problem with these self-cures is that they are familiar—
available reassurances—and that, in a sense, they work, so they
never change (so intractable are they that people end up making
"I am the kind of person who" statements, which are usually
descriptions of their inhibitions). These defenses work by sub-
stituting a more tolerable form of suffering for something
deemed to be intolerable; and they work by concealing the
truth of the predicament to minimize the immediacy of its im-
pact. So the most difficult task for the analyst, as Masud Khan
remarked, is curing the patient's self-cure.[5] A second chance,
however, may be a viable self-cure.

The symptom as repeated, compulsive self-cure becomes
an addiction to what can be called the first chance (the time
and place and situation in which it all started), and to the fear
of second chances as too disruptive, as threatening to retrau-
matize the patient. As though to remove or modify the patients'
symptoms is to leave them literally defenseless; to expose them
again to the original trauma. When a second chance is not felt
to be an inviting opportunity, it is felt to be a terror. The second chance always exposes us, once again, to the risks of the
first chance. The unknown future that the second chance offers is preempted and replaced by the known future that the
first chance left us with. The second chance, however attractive
it may seem, is news that never stays news.

We all have our personal repertoires, however unconscious, of so-called symptoms, of what to do (or say) when, of
how to manage whatever is disturbing us. And so it is not surprising that however hampered we might be by our symptom-
atic self-cures, we would feel radically unprotected without
them. So symptoms, like habits, are the enemies of the second
chance. And this is partly because we cannot imagine that this—
this missing of people, this fear of conflict—could possibly be
done differently without putting ourselves in mortal danger.

"The ego treats recovery itself as a new danger," Freud writes, because recovery—the modification or abolishing of symptoms, the proving of their irrelevance—is equated with the initial and initiating trauma, and the resourcelessness felt in the face of it. It is a traumatic memory that is being recovered, in the service of a larger recovery. What from the outside might look like a (more pleasurable, more enlivening) second chance—the enjoyment of longing, say, the inspiration of disagreement—feels like an unknown and unknowable and therefore inaccessible and threatening possibility (we who have not had a second wind yet don't quite know how to get one except by continuing to do what we are doing). We only have second chances because we have heard them spoken of, and they must be made to sound alluring because, Freud believes, we are predisposed to fear them. When the second chance is unappealing it sounds like more of the same but worse.

What Freud is saying is, Never underestimate the fear, the faith, the confidence that belief in the second chance (of recovery) always entails. We know what the consequences of our first chances were; we know the ways we have evolved of managing danger and of recognizing what we feel endangered by (first chances—the original situation—are the devil we think we know). But by the same token we can never know where the second chance will take us; the second chance involves us in the unknown and unknowable future that is craved and feared (there is a real sense in which believing in the second chance is the way of believing in a future, or in a future worth wanting). A second chance is always a redescription of a first chance, but with unknown consequences. Because for Freud, as we have seen, the second chance is always a reworking of our first experiences of danger. The second chance, that is to say, always reminds us of a trauma. And it is indeed of interest—though it is typically psychoanalytic—to describe our first chances, albeit implicitly, as our first chance to manage what endangers us, and to manage what we wanted, the two things all too often going together.

The fear then, or anxiety, the need or desire of childhood is, in the Freudian story, our first chance. But our first chance for what? At its crudest we could say, our first chance is for survival; which means surviving our initial (and initiating) need and the environment we find to meet it. It contains what we need and want, and whoever is looking after us. So in our early life there is our first chance for survival, and our first chance for enjoyment, for the pleasure of nurture, of being relieved of unhappiness, and for the pleasure of pleasure. Our ongoing survival takes the form of our development, what Winnicott calls "the imaginative elaboration of physical function."[6] We can assume—and indeed observe in children—that there is a kind of primal pleasure in our own development, in our growing capacity to do things. Development is one chance after another for the child to master fears and pleasures and disappointments. And yet quite soon, as Freud intimates, the child settles into a relatively fixed pattern, a repertoire of what we can call defenses, all the essentially self-protective inhibitions that keep the child, he believes, sufficiently safe. And this is where and when the second chance becomes an option: after the first chance has proved itself to be unbearably frustrating.

The child may keep on growing, but the growth is always tempered by the character armor of his or her defenses, by the child's strategies for self-protection, which tend to consolidate rather than change. Each developmental stage—infancy, latency, puberty, and so on—has, in the Freudian story, its own more or less recognizable set of defenses. But there is a paradox at the heart of the psychoanalytic story about growing up—the child develops, but the child's defenses tend not to. Indeed,

Freud shows how much people grow into their defenses rather than out of them. So when it comes to second chances—in psychoanalytic language, the recovery of feeling and desire through the modification of defenses—people are extremely selective about the second chances they are willing to contemplate or consider. One of the things we often determinedly do not want to know about ourselves is what would count for us as a second chance in any given predicament.

Second chances are risks, and everyone has a more or less unconscious repertoire of significant risks. The first chance, in the Freudian story—the opportunity for gratification of need, signaled by fear and anxiety—is met with an inhibition; the second chance—provided by psychoanalytic treatment—is, in the words of the psychoanalyst Roger Money-Kyrle, to show the irrelevance of the inhibition.[7] The original scenario can be reworked, the formative fears can be redescribed, a second chance can evolve out of a first chance. And yet Freud kept finding, as I say, that what he called "the resistance" "finally brings work to a halt."[8] A second chance turns out to be the first and the last thing the patient wants. The possibility of the second chance always has in it the fear of the second chance. The second chance always has within it—however much it is denied, or refused, or set to one side—a fantasy of catastrophe. The defensive solutions to the first chances are meant to preempt the possibility of there being a second chance. They are meant to be final (and finalizing) solutions. Where there was once a shock or a disturbance there must now be a reliably repeated way of meeting it, like a question that always comes with its answer. Any defensive measure that needed to be given a second chance could not be deemed trustworthy. Defenses are only worth having if they are reliable. But like overprotective parents, they starve the child in the name of safety.

＊

For a second chance, then, to be a second chance, something
is repeated with a view to innovation and improvement (a second chance is, in this sense, at once an improvisation and an
innovation). It is, that is to say, the opposite, the antidote to any
kind of repetition compulsion, or trauma; it replaces a mecha-
nism with an intention; I stop repeating myself, as I do when
traumatized (or intimidated), I recover the intention of doing
something different. And I can do something different because
I have been able to redescribe what has happened to me in a
way that opens it up (as Leontes can do in *The Winter's Tale*,
and as Shakespeare's tragic heroes can never do). What felt like
a fate has become a choice. And whatever else the idea of the
second chance does, it restores our confidence in choice making. Second chances, then, as a cure for repetition, for the automatic and the mechanical; second chances as an alternative
to any of the available determinisms. (When Jean-Paul Sartre
famously wrote, "I am my choices," he was saying that there is
always a second chance.)

Freud describes second chances as the getting over or
through a resistance, which involves the revaluing of an initially
traumatizing desire and situation. And yet what is striking in
Freud's account, as we can see, is that what we might call first
chances—which second chances are there to revise—are always
traumatic. Whereas for what became known in psychoanalysis
as object-relations theory—in which relationship rather than
instinct was deemed to be formative—needing and wanting and
desiring were only as traumatic as the initial objects of desire—
the parents—made them (the child who has to wait too long to
be fed experiences her or his hunger as traumatic). For Freud
and others of his followers, needing and wanting and desiring
are intrinsically traumatic. Jean Laplanche writes of "the attack

of the drives on the ego" as though instinct at once sustains and destabilizes the individual.[9] We cannot live without desiring, but desiring endangers us.

Home is not where we start from; fear is where we start from.

The first chance always, by definition, determines what is taken to be a second chance. If the first chance is taken to be essentially traumatic, as it is for Freud, the descriptions of the second chance are likely to veer between the redemptive and revolutionary (the magical dissolution of the trauma, apocalyptic renewal) and the cautious and conservative (improvement without radical transformation, the more modest pleasure of reform, the consolations of small changes). If psychoanalysis was to be the science of second chances—was to be a respectable and legitimate medical treatment—it had to be careful about what it promised. The kind of second chances provided by psychoanalysis, Freud was keen to insist, were anti-religious and so anti-redemptive. The claims made by Freud about psychoanalysis were neither grandiose nor revolutionary: Freud never claimed to be making new kinds of people, or to be converting anyone to anything. When Freud suggested, for example, that the aim of psychoanalysis was to transform hysterical misery into ordinary human unhappiness he was not promising his patients the earth.[10] He *was* saying, though, that ordinary human unhappiness could be an object of desire, that ordinary human unhappiness could itself be a second chance, if only for patients suffering from hysteria. Something has to be described as a second chance in order to be one. And Freud was here giving ordinary human unhappiness a second chance too. Just as when he suggested that psychoanalysis could improve a person's capacity to love and work, Freud was always promoting bourgeois values but with a twist of something else. After all, if one were to have the second chance of improving one's capacity to love and work, what might that actually entail? How would one like to improve one's capacity to love and work? What would it take to do that?

It was, then, part of Freud's goal in the invention of psychoanalysis to redescribe the whole notion of second chances in what he took to be their most realistic, but still imaginative, forms. By asking what the modern individual could hope for, Freud was asking what the available and sustaining satisfactions were. As a determined antidote to the second chances that formed and informed Freud's Judeo-Christian world—the second chances of being converted, of being saved, of there being an afterlife, not to mention the secular second chance of assimilation—psychoanalysis wanted to offer realistic hope; something that seemed a contradiction in terms of what Freud saw as our all-too-wishful selves. And realistic hope meant working out what, if anything, our second chances might be. As though Freud wanted psychoanalysis to be religion's second chance, and wanted to give second chances a chance by preventing them from being forms of magical thinking.

Given that our first chances were so troubled and troubling, what would our second chances look like? It was a question that involved Freud in an even more confounding question: What would our instinctual life be like—and of course the defenses it seems to necessitate—when it is given a second chance, the second chance provided by the redescriptions of psychoanalysis? What would it be, from a psychoanalytic point of view, to be cured? Freud was suggesting that we can give our instinctual life—or our lives as instinctual creatures—a second chance through psychoanalytic treatment. But what kind of life, in other words, do those cured by psychoanalysis—by the second chance of psychoanalysis—live? In what sense is the idea of second chances applicable to the Freudian picture of ourselves as Darwinian desiring creatures? If the Darwinian word for second chances is, in a sense, *adaptation*—and Freud does propose that we can and should be better adapted to our instinctual life lived in what he called "civilization"—the Freudian word for second chances may be *psychoanalysis.*

"One day in winter," Proust writes in *Swann's Way,*

> on my return home, my mother, seeing that I was cold, offered me some tea, a thing I did not ordinarily take. I declined at first, and then for no particular reason, changed my mind. She sent for one of those squat, plump little cakes called "petites madeleines." . . . No sooner had the warm liquid mixed with the crumbs touched my palate than a shiver ran through me and I stopped, intent upon the extraordinary thing that was happening to me.[11]

It is, we should note, Marcel's giving himself a second chance— "I declined at first, and then for no particular reason, changed my mind"—that makes the second chance, that is, Proustian involuntary memory, possible. Through his being offered something he did not usually have, which he at first refused, he is flooded with enlivening memories. But what Proust insists upon in his description of this famous event is that it need not have happened. An accidental configuration of intentions and circumstances conjured a life-changing event that became the emblem of Proust's book and his writing of it.

Whether or not he was in search of lost time, his incidental tasting of the madeleine brought it back to him. He was certainly not (consciously) searching for lost time when he decided to eat the cake; the whole experience might easily have been missed. Though once it happens, once it happens to happen, he relishes it. "There is a large element of chance in these matters," Proust writes, "and a second chance occurrence, that of our own death, often prevents us from awaiting for any length of time the favours of the first."[12] Death is only a chance occurrence in the sense that we know that we will die but not when and where. It is a strange construction: the first chance—or rather, chance event—is the involuntary memory inspired by the madeleine; the second chance is death, which puts a final end to such chance occurrences. If death is, as it were, the second chance here, it is an unusual one; we do not usually—but perhaps we should—think of second chances as the end of something. And yet the invocation of chance here reminds us of the unarranged, of everything that is—in psychoanalytic language—beyond our omnipotence, and of how, when we talk of second chances, it can be all too easy to think of them as both somehow arranged and always potentially productive. If the idea of second chances tends to reinforce our sense of agency, of our capacity to make choices, Proust's particular insistence on chance renders us as simply the recipients of second chances. In his case the second chance that is memory. And he also wants to remind us that a second chance might be putting a stop to something; perhaps, in the case of dying, of course, putting a stop to something forever.

Our death will finally put an end to the possibility of these gratuitous encounters, these accidents, in which we find ourselves recovering lost time, whether we want to or not. And once his past experiences are given the second chance of being unexpectedly and unexpectingly remembered—as happens several times in the novel—Marcel is fascinated and intrigued and enlivened: "a shiver ran through me," rather like an orgasm, and he felt it to be an extraordinary thing that was happening. You can sometimes feel in this very long novel that Marcel, however busy he is, is more or less biding his time in the hope that one of these accidental revelations of memory will occur.

As though these epiphany-like experiences are his real object of desire. He is given a kind of second chance in these extraordinary moments when the past is given a second chance by being suddenly remembered. It is as though Marcel feels himself to be losing his life in the passing of time, and in every sporadic influx of memory he is recovering something of himself. He reconstitutes himself through memory, something he has no control over; he is reassembled by memory without his being able to do the reassembling. It just happens to him. But so much of the past—which seems to be lying in wait for him—is lost forever. It is the second chance given by memory that makes past experience real. But the past, which is essentially what vitalizes the present for Proust, is by definition always elusive. "It is a labour in vain to attempt to recapture it," he writes, "all the efforts of our intellect must prove futile. The past is hidden somewhere outside the realm, beyond the reach of intellect, in some material object (in the sensation which that material object will give us) of which we have no inkling. And it depends on chance whether or not we come upon this object before we ourselves must die."[13]

It is as though in Proust's account of memory there are two second chances in play, one leading to the other, and both impossible to organize. There is the unwitting second chance of eating the madeleine which leads to the second second chance of remembering the past; eating the madeleine is not known to be a second chance, but the memories evoked are recognized as giving Marcel the second chance of reexperiencing and re-describing his lost past. One second chance precipitates another. For Proust, there is the story of the second chance and the story generated by the second chance. Proust does not say that we have to be alert or receptive to our second chances, simply that second chances do happen to us, and they should be recognized as such, because there is a real sense in which we only come to life in our second chances. There's a lot in them, not least of which is what they tell us about our first chances; and they redeem our losses. The one thing we know about our first chances, as we have said, is that they are to all intents and purposes lost—discarded, derisively rejected, gone missing, vanished, or simply dead—until, that is, they are remembered, if only by chance.

Freud says we work to forget our first chances; Proust says that we await their recovery. They agree that the first chances that make the idea of second chances intelligible have to be remembered. Freud invents a method for remembering and reconstructing our first chances that can make second chances possible. Proust believes we can have no say in how and what we remember; but that the second chance *is* the remembering, the vitalizing and fortifying power of memory. For Freud, memory, the undoing of repression, is in the service of more truth and satisfaction; for Proust, memory has no discernible or organized project or program but is its own reward (it does, though, break what he calls "the anaesthetic effect of habit").[14] If we are lucky enough to have the second chance of remembering something from the past, it is the pleasure and exhilaration of this second chance that suffices, as though our aliveness is in certain of our memories. Freud knows what our second chances should be for; Proust does not, and could not, though it is their effect on him that he prizes. For Proust it is the word *chance* we should take seriously in the phrase "second chance." For Proust second chances are pieces of luck with no defining, discernible purpose; for Freud second chances only matter because of what we can do with them, and what they can do for us.

If, as we have said, a first chance can confer a kind of freshness—a pure singularity—upon experience, then we can see both Freud and Proust wanting to recover something of this initial and initiating freshness and yet suggesting that this freshness is only fully realized—or lived, or appreciated, or recognized, or properly acknowledged and celebrated—in its re-currence as a second chance. As though the pure singularity of the first chance is only fully disclosed in its revival as a second chance. As though something was lost and needed a deferred recovery to come fully to life.

Our sense of what a second chance is for us can only come from the past. So a second chance is at once a memory and a prophecy, a recollection and a hope. But what constitutes a chance—to be taken or to be shied away from—is not always clear; nor is it altogether clear what calling a chance a second chance adds to the situation. Freud and Proust clearly want us to think about our second chances, and what they might be there for. Why, that is to say, the idea of revision is so compelling, and what it might inspire in us. Why second chances are all too often the chances we most want, as though by being second chances they may be the chances we are most able to take.

So both Freud and Proust, then, make us wonder whether second chances—as we might wonder about memories—are made or just happen to be found. Whether a second chance is an artifact, or something simply there to be discovered. That is to say, once you begin to believe in second chances, once you start to want them, what is to be done?

7

Second Chances

For and Against

Kafka's "Leopards in the Temple" is a parable about, among other things, second chances; both what they are for, and how they sometimes work. The story begins with a novel act of violence, of trauma, which is then turned into something else, the something else that is like a second chance. As if to say, some second chances might be as much about adaptation as about renovation, as much about coming to terms with something as about changing things; that adaptation may require improvisation as well as compliance if it is to work as any kind of second chance. But the point of the parable is that the initial trauma can be turned into a second chance: "Leopards break into the temple and drink to the dregs what is in the sacrificial pitchers; this is repeated over and over again; finally it can be calculated in advance, and it becomes a part of the ceremony."[1]

It is as though both the leopards and the temple are given a second chance; but the second chance, in this case, is an act of normalization; the bizarre becomes ordinary, a violation becomes a norm. What apparently disrupted the ritual has become part of the ritual. It has been included, not defended against (there is no punishment involved). In this second chance the original trauma becomes a significant contribution; something utterly unanticipated, once it can be relied on—"calculated in advance"—is made integral. The leopards breaking into the temple may have been experienced by the worshippers, if not by the leopards, as a rupture, but they are incorporated into the ritual. In the psychoanalyst Robert Stoller's phrase—describing the project in so-called sexual perversions—this is a second chance as a "turning of trauma into triumph"; any sense of loss or catastrophe is averted.[2] Where there was defeatedness there is now a kind of renewal. Where there was essentially the shock of the new, there is revision. Whatever else they are, second chances are then an attempt to turn disturbing experiences into a viable future. Indeed, what is recovered in second chances is the future, the future as desirable, or at least viable. So what happens, say, to the developing child—and puberty is perhaps the most vivid example of this—is that leopards keep breaking into the temple; or this would be another parallel suggested by the parable. At each developmental stage hard-won accom-modations and adaptations are disrupted by new experiences, as new appetites (and accidents) displace old ones, and first chances are given another chance. The point of Kafka's parable is not simply the disruption but rather the absorption or trans-formation of the disruption into the ritual.

The first chance forecloses something—or is used to fore-close something; the second chance is a reopening, a recovery of potential. And yet what the parable suggests—and what makes it a parable—is that second chances are always equivocal, un-certain in their consequences, and ambiguous in their mean-ing. They are never an uncomplicated good; they never release us into a predictable narrative of what happens next. We can-not know how this new ritual in the temple will play out, nor what might change it, nor what the effect of these leopards on

any individual worshipper might be. The second chance, like
the first chance, has to unfold over time. The shock of the new
guarantees nothing. Because we do not speak of third or fourth
or fifth chances we are tempted to assume that the second
chance may be the last chance. Or the last chance we need.

So to be simply exhilarated or reassured, or even intrigued,
by the idea of the second chance is often to underestimate the
sense in which the idea of the second chance may be as much
of an alibi, say, as an opportunity (we tend not to ask what
a second chance may be an avoidance of). Because the idea of
second chances can also be something we use to free ourselves
from certain constraints—like a password to some kind of freedom, or agency, or independence: to a life of our own—we may
need to be sometimes suspicious of what we are using, or wanting, the whole notion of second chances to do for us. There is
a temptation, that is to say, to recruit second chances too exclusively for our vocabulary of optimism, which always runs
the risk of oversimplifying them, not doing them justice. The
second chance that the future might hold also allows us, in ways
that are not always easy to acknowledge, to imagine ourselves
floating free of our immediate circumstances and predicaments.
Second chances, then, are exploitable in a way that first chances
are often not; they link us to our options rather than linking us
to our losses, which are the reason second chances are required.
If I know I can read this book again, how much do I really need
to concentrate? If I can always rely on being given a second
chance by my wife, my friend, my God, in what sense do my
misdemeanors really matter? If this relationship is frustrating
there is always another one (promiscuity is compulsive second
chancing). So what we gain in freedom by taking second chances
for granted we may lose in commitment or engagement or at-
tentiveness; what we gain in relief we may lose in what used to
be called seriousness (when I am absorbed in someone or some-

thing, second chances disappear as a preoccupation). If there are second chances available we can afford to be distracted, we can experiment with (or risk) failure, we can fob ourselves off by believing that we can always redeem the time. And, of course, all this may also be no bad thing. But when second chances loom we can keep our eye on the exit. We need to notice, in other words, also what we are delegating to the longed-for second chance.

We may be driven by our instincts, we may be the victims of formative childhood trauma, we may be, to all intents and purposes the ventriloquists' dummies of the languages and codes we are born into; and yet Freud and his followers, as the inheritors of the Enlightenment and of Romanticism, could not help but be interested in the idea of freedom. The poet Stéphane Mallarmé's "basic question," Sartre wrote, was, "Can we ever find within determinism a way out of it?"[3] This too was to be Freud's question in his invention of psychoanalysis: In what sense, given the multiple determinisms of our lives— of biology, of language, of economics, of politics, of class—do we have the capacity to make choices, second chances reintroducing the idea of agency into psychoanalysis? If psychoanalysis, like all the modern therapies—and, indeed, the religions that were their precursors—offers people a second chance, an opportunity to remake their lives, what is actually being proposed? Freud veers between a "Leopards in the Temple" account of freedom—second chances involving finding ways of making a virtue of necessity, of fashioning a future from trauma—and intimating that there is nothing more wishful, more improbably omnipotent than believing that there are second chances in life. Freud's commitment to second chances, then, discussed in an earlier chapter, needs to be measured against his profound ambivalence about the possibilities for change; the sense, which recurs in Freud's writing, that we may endorse second chances—

indeed the second chance provided by psychoanalytic treatment—
but we need to be skeptical. Freud often also wants to tell us that
second chances may need to be ironized as well as celebrated.
Things can sometimes be improved, Freud believes, but they
cannot be redeemed. It will be the work of Winnicott, as we
shall see, to bring something akin to the idea of redemption
into psychoanalytic theory and practice. For Winnicott, development in childhood depends on second chances. So we now
need to look at Winnicott's account of what he calls the antisocial tendency in children as an initial elaboration of his ongoing sense of the effects and consequences of maternal absence
referred to earlier.

In thinking about second chances, at least to begin with,
it may be worth wondering—in a way that Freud helps us to
do—what a life would be like in which there were no such thing,
a life in which every act was irredeemable (in which apology
would be nonsensical), every transgression unforgiven and un-
forgivable (in which mercy would be unrealistic), every mistake uncorrectable (in which revision would be impossible),
every act and apparent choice determined by forces beyond
us. A life in which losses could not be recovered, and conflicts
could not be resolved. A life without cure or hope or useful repetition (after all, within a life there may often be second chances,
but there is no second chance of having a life). So how, then,
would our lives be different—or even better—if we lived as if
there were no such thing as a second chance? It is an almost
impossible question to answer, but it is something many people have had to do. It would be a life spent adapting to an absolute defeatedness, a life of intractable guilt and irredeemable
shame. It could feel like a life of radical self-betrayal. This is
why so-called growing up, in its psychoanalytic accounts, involves working out where in our lives we can have, or be given,

a second chance. And what to do when second chances are not available.

And yet, clearly, when we think of ourselves as "dependent rational animals," in the philosopher Alasdair MacIntyre's useful phrase, we tend not to think of ourselves as quite so dependent on our belief in second chances as we in fact are.[4] But a life without second chances, on consideration, is, if not virtually inconceivable, a life not obviously worth living; they are an essential, taken for granted part of our lives, or of the way we think about our lives. As though we cannot bear to think of our lives, to describe our lives, as unimprovable. As though we can only do things in the knowledge that we could do them better, or at least do them again (we would not, as children, want to be stuck with our spelling mistakes). Indeed, whenever we are thinking of freedom or possibility or choice, in personal and political terms, we have to recruit, in one way or another, our faith in second chances. We have to be able to believe that we are not imprisoned in the moment; that there is, as we say, room for improvement.

Whether as bad faith—I can do this better later—or as the making of amends—I can fix this—the idea of the second chance gives us a chance; it puts time on our side; we can reverse it, replay it, redo it. We can use it rather than be victimized by it. It gives us space and time and opportunity; it lets us think, and discuss things (what would conversation be like in a world without second chances?). We can mend the past in the present and the future. This is what our hope is based on. And we can see this anxiety, this uncertainty about what is possible, about what we can recover, what we can realistically hope for, being worked out, in the language of psychoanalysis, among many other places. When Freud writes about what he calls "the repetition compulsion" and Winnicott writes about the "good-enough mothering" development as possible undeclared alternatives to both compulsion and repetition, they are wondering what place, if any, freedom and agency and choice and pleasure might have in the deterministic theories they abide by (theories about our lives as instinct driven, bent on survival and reproduction, and subject to an ineluctable life cycle).[5] And they are wondering what we are doing when we are doing something again, or when we think we are, or when we want to or cannot help but do it. They are writing, in other words, about second chances. Freedom, perhaps unsurprisingly, is not a psychoanalytic term; but it is freedom, and its secret sharer the second chance, that are at stake when we are talking about repetition, and about play, and about the future; and indeed about pleasure and satisfaction. At its most minimal, psychoanalysis suggests that knowing what we cannot help but be constrained by is the precondition for taking our chances. And everything depends on what we take to be a chance, and whether we can take it.

It is in *Beyond the Pleasure Principle* (1920) that Freud writes about the compulsion to repeat and children's play. In what became an iconic scene in the history of psychoanalysis Freud described in the famous "fort-da" example, a game he observed his one-and-a-half-year-old grandson playing, a little boy he describes as "greatly attached to his mother," and therefore greatly troubled by her absences. "This good little boy," he writes,

> had an occasional disturbing habit of taking any small objects he could get hold of and throwing them away from him into a corner, under the bed, and so on, so that hunting for his toys and picking them up was often quite a business. As he did this he gave vent to a long and drawn out "o-o-o-o" accompa-

nied by an expression of interest and satisfaction. His mother and the writer of the present account were agreed in thinking that this was not a mere interjection but represented the German word "fort" [gone]. I eventually realised that this was a game and that the only use he made of any of his toys was to play "gone" with them. One day I made an observation which confirmed my view. The child had a wooden reel with a piece of string tied around it. It never occurred to him to pull it along the floor behind him, for instance, and play at its being a carriage. What he did was to hold the reel by the string, and very skilfully throw it over the edge of the curtained cot, so that it disappeared into it, at the same time uttering his expressive "o-o-o-o." He then pulled the reel out of the cot again by the string and hailed its reappearance with a joyful "da" [there]. This, then, was the complete game—disappearance and return. . . . The interpretation of the game then became obvious. It was related to the child's great cultural achievement, the instinctual renunciation (that is, the renunciation of instinctual satisfaction) which he had made in allowing his mother to go away without protesting. He compensated himself for this, as it were, by himself staging the disappearance and return of the objects within his reach. . . . The child cannot possibly have felt his mother's departure as something agreeable or even indifferent.[6]

The child is described as having two experiences: the mother's departure, after her presence, which he must endure, and his symbolic reconstruction of this departure in a game (the first time as tragedy, the second time as play). (Or, to continue the

"Leopard" allegory, as ritual.) The child has managed to do two
things—he has apparently mastered, symbolically, what was in-
flicted upon him, taking control of something that was beyond
his control (in Freud's language he has turned passive into active). And he has turned pain into pleasure, he has transformed
something he had to suffer into something he is able to enjoy
(it is the child's pleasure that Freud is notably impressed by).
Through his game he recovers his delight in living, and his confidence in his mother. But this is a success story, a progress
myth—not unlike Kafka's parable—that begs more questions
than it answers.

As Freud makes clear, there is a sense in which the child
is also telling himself a lie, through the invention of the game.
The child gives himself a second chance to experience the
mother's absence as something he is pleasurably in charge of,
and can more than bear. But the second chance is used to con-
ceal the truth of the first chance, a truth which it is assumed the
child cannot bear—that the mother whom he needs is independent of his need. That he is utterly dependent on someone
over whom he has limited control. As in "Leopards in the Temple," this is a story, as I say, about making a virtue of necessity.
The second chance, the game he invents, is a cover story for,
and an interpretation of, the initial and initiating experience. It
is a solution that brings its own problems. The second chance
as a wonderful invention, a testament to acculturation and to
the child's great cultural achievement, that is at the same time
an unwillingness or an inability to straightforwardly face the
truth (the child does not have the mother he needs under remote control, or any other kind of control). The child's terror
is both contained and dissipated by the game ("we have art that
we may not perish of the truth," Nietzsche famously remarked,
and this Freud redescribes). Freud presents us with the second
chance as displacement, as evasion, as "compensation," and as

liberation. And as refuge from the actuality of the first chance, the chance to experience the mother's separateness, in all its terrible and bewildering immediacy. The imaginative rework-ing of experience through play here is a way of surviving and enjoying an unavoidable suffering. The child has to gradually come to terms with the fact that the mother has a life of her own. So Freud wants us to see that the second chance—that is, the game—has a lot of work to do, and that without it the child would be, in the fullest sense, abandoned. That second chances may always be more complicated, more disturbingly enigmatic, than they look. A second chance can be a strange and unnerv-ing promise.

Freud's view here is that play is the child's second chance to deal with the overwhelming intensity and immediacy of ex-perience, of the founding experience of the child's relationship with the mother; play as the self-cure for trauma, the second chance as the self-cure for the first. "It is clear," Freud writes, "that in their play children repeat everything that has made a great impression on them in real life, and that in doing so they abreact the strength of the impression and, as one might put it, make themselves master of the situation."[7] And, as one might put it, children make themselves the master of an experience that they cannot be the master of. The second chance as mas-tery clearly puts the second chance into question. The child's great cultural achievement is based on an illusion, on an om-nipotence that has never, and could never have, existed. And it is worth wondering what second chances might be if they are not attempted acts of mastery, or, indeed, disguised forms of masochism in which suffering is survived (again) by being made pleasurable the second time round. Once again it is the second chance that realizes—that makes real and reveals the potential of—the first chance. Reveals both how disturbing the first chance was, and how full of concealed possibility. It is the disappearing mother that makes the child creative. It is the taking and the making of a second chance—with all its bewildering history—that the child's survival depends upon. The need that most needs to be acknowledged is the need for a second chance. Only the omnipotent, we might think, only God can live without second chances. And, Freud adds, only the omnipotent need to believe in them. It is the omnipotent part of the child that makes and takes his second chance. In making up his game he makes up, and makes up for, a lot.

There is, then, for Freud the complicated repetition—of trauma, of strong impressions—of play, and of play as second chance for the child to at once manage, survive, and experience his experience. And then there are the more mechanistic (machinelike) workings of what he calls the repetition compulsion, which by definition dispels the whole notion of second chances (a compulsion is something that is beyond choice and cannot be revised). "The compulsion to repeat," Jean Laplanche and Jean-Bertrand Pontalis write,

> is an ungovernable process originating in the unconscious. As a result of its action, the subject deliberately places himself in distressing situations, thereby repeating an old experience, but he does not recall this prototype; on the contrary, he has the strong impression that the situation is fully determined by the circumstances of the moment. . . . It is seen, in the final analysis, as the expression of the most general character of the instincts, namely, their conservatism.[8]

If the instincts, which supposedly determine our lives, are inherently conservative and ungovernable, then fundamental change, fundamental revision is impossible. Nobody, in this story, gets a second chance when it comes to instinctual life. There may be minor modifications—modifications made, say, by psychoanalytic treatment, or by other relationships and accidents—but what might be called our essential (biological) selves are immutable (we keep returning to the same distressing situations). The repetition compulsion, that is to say, makes a mockery of the idea of second chances, and, of course, of the idea of our being in any sense the authors of our own lives: freedom and autonomy and the making of choices are the first casualties of the life sentence that is the repetition compulsion. Or, to put it another way, in the Freudian story there are the good—the beneficial, the enlivening, the inspiring, the fortifying—repetitions, like his grandson's game, that are potentially second chances; and there are the anti–second chances of the repetition compulsion. The repetition compulsion at its starkest requires of us that we be resigned to our fate. That we learn to coexist with forces beyond our control.

So in trying to define the repetition compulsion, Laplanche and Pontalis ask, quite sensibly, "What is the tendency towards repetition a function of?":

> Is it a matter of attempts made by the ego, in a piecemeal fashion, to master and abreact excessive tensions? Repetitive dreams following mental traumas would especially tend to bear this out. Or must we accept the idea that repetition has, in the last analysis, to be related to the most "instinctual" part—the "daemonic" aspect—of every instinct—to that tendency towards absolute discharge which is implied by the notion of the death instinct?[9]

Repetition is presented here as mastery and evacuation, Freud's notion of the so-called death instinct referring to a supposed part of the self that wants to kill the individual's vitality (and freedom, such as it is). Second chances, we must assume, are usually presumed to be on the side of a person's aliveness, and freedom, an appetite for what Nietzsche called "more life." By invoking the idea of the daemonic—of a life possessed rather than a life of choices—Freud's work sounds less modern, less secular, more allied with the pagan and the supernatural. And this momentarily highlights the sense in which the idea of second chances is going to be available only in certain cultures, in certain vocabularies. Clearly, in the light of the repetition compulsion there can be no place for chances of any kind.

With his ideas of the repetition compulsion and the death instinct, then, Freud was inviting us to imagine a life that we cannot enhance or ameliorate, a life without the reality of second chances; or he is, at its most minimal, helping us to imagine what the promise of second chances might have to contend with—we may know that in our second chances we are often up against it, but we do not always know what in ourselves may be against *them*. With his ideas about children's play as a kind of loophole, Freud wanted us to think of play as the child's second chance to survive her or his experience, and of second chances as compensations or substitute satisfactions for inevitable suffering, for the cumulative trauma that is childhood. And the child who can play is not under the sway of the repetition-compulsion.

Freud wants us to acknowledge how desperate and repetitive we are, and how impoverished—perhaps unsurprisingly in such a context—our vocabulary of revision is. Pretending to master the unmasterable is, to put it mildly, an ironic description of a second chance (as is another of his images, of the individual directing the horse in the direction the horse wants to go). Mastery, truthfulness, realism, and compromise tend to be Freud's solutions to the rigors of living. And yet, of course,

Freud's theory is usefully at odds with his practice. After all, what is psychoanalytic treatment if not the possibility of a second chance for a person's growth and development and satisfaction? The unconscious, as Freud describes it, could be conceived of as a second chance for the inevitable dessications of consciousness; just as the dream, in its re-presentation of desire, gives our instinctual life a second chance, an opportunity to be reconsidered. The repetition compulsion itself may invite redescription and revision (as it did, for example, in existentialism; if, in Sartre's words, "I am my choices," the repetition compulsion has been demystified and discarded). But Freud, when he is writing about what might seem like second chances, is more likely to ironize than to celebrate. Freud is always skeptical of our assertions of freedom, of our claims, as he puts it, to be masters in our own houses. The idea of second chances, by implying that we can make our lives more the way we want them to be, fosters the sense that our lives, to some extent, can be our own.

It would be in the appropriately named Independent Group in British psychoanalysis—one of whose members, Marion Milner, wrote a remarkable book titled *A Life of One's Own*—that second chances came into their own in psychoanalysis.[10] If Freud taught us to be skeptical of what we want to call second chances, it was Winnicott who saw the uses of their being worked, tacitly, into a psychoanalytic account of a life and celebrated.

A second chance is defined by the *Longman Dictionary of Contemporary English* as "help given to someone who has failed, in the hope that they will succeed this time."[11] It is a phrase that is notably not usually cited in other, more traditional contemporary dictionaries, perhaps because it is too contemporary—that is, it is an idea we need in contemporary life. And it is deemed to be a possible solution to failure, but possibly failure as a kind

of precondition for a different kind of success. Or rather, it is
not clear whether, or in what sense, it is implied in the definition that a success that is not born of a second chance is in any
way better than one that is. It is clear, though, that second chances
are about hope, about restoring hope.

When Winnicott writes about delinquency, he is writing
about hope and failure. In his remarkable developmental theory, delinquency is always a sign of hope in a child, and the
child's delinquent behavior is understood to be the child's second chance to meet and mend an earlier deprivation. In Winnicott's story, first the child is and feels deprived; this is the story
of some kind of maternal "failure," a failure, that is, from the
child's point of view; and then, reactive to this loss or absence
of something essential—the child having to survive, say, a de-
pressed mother—the child enacts an attempted self-cure. In
a paper of that name Winnicott describes what he calls "the
antisocial tendency," using as an example a child who steals a
bicycle as part of a self-cure:

> The antisocial tendency is characterized by an ele-
> ment in it which compels the environment to be
> important. The patient through unconscious drives
> compels someone to attend to management. . . . *The
> antisocial tendency implies hope.* Lack of hope is the
> basic feature of the deprived child. . . . In the period
> of hope the child manifests an antisocial tendency.
> This may be awkward for society, and for you if it is
> your bicycle that is stolen. . . . When there is an an-
> tisocial tendency there has been a true deprivation
> (not a simple privation); that is to say, there has been
> a loss of something good that has been positive in
> the child's experience up to a certain date, and that
> has been withdrawn; the withdrawal has extended

over a period of time longer than that over which
the child can keep the memory of the experience
alive.[12]

Winnicott is describing a process here: the child's first chance,
so to speak, is of being provided with what she or he needs—
what Winnicott calls "the good-enough mothering"—for the
child's own development, which is then withdrawn. The child
then alerts her- or himself and the environment to this deprivation through an antisocial act by means of which the child
hopes, unconsciously, that this deprivation will be recognized,
and hopes to make up for the deprivation in symbolic form
(the child does not really need a bicycle, she or he needs maternal care, needs this deprivation understood and to some
extent met). The antisocial act is the child's attempt to be given
a second chance at development, as though the child's delinquency was a kind of unconscious performance art for the parents, or for anyone willing to be sufficiently attentive. When a
child steals, that child is, in Winnicott's view, stealing a symbolic
substitute for what she or he feels deprived of, and felt entitled
to (babies do not steal from their mothers, Winnicott reminds
us). "Stealing is at the centre of the antisocial tendency," Winnicott writes,

> with the associated lying. The child who steals an
> object is not looking for the object stolen but seeks
> the mother over whom he or she has rights. These
> rights derive from the fact that (from the child's point
> of view) the mother was [initially] created by the
> child. . . . The manifestation of the antisocial tendency
> includes stealing and lying, incontinence and the
> making of a mess generally. Although each symp-
> tom has its specific meaning and value, the common

factor for my purpose in my attempt to describe the
antisocial tendency is the nuisance value of the symptoms. This nuisance value is exploited by the child,
and is not a chance affair. Much of the motivation is
unconscious, but not necessarily all.[13]

In this story the child originally creates the mother in fantasy,
the gratifying and reliable mother who comes when the child
needs her. When she becomes the depriving mother she becomes too real—beyond the range of the child's omnipotent
fantasy, an independent person—and has to be recovered as
the mother over whom the child has rights through the second chance of the antisocial act (in Winnicott's view the child
has—in a provocative use of the word—the right to, and rights
over, the mother she or he needs for her or his own development). So children who steal are alerting the environment to
the fact that there is something they need that they cannot get,
and that there is no one who will collaborate with them to recognize their needs and get those needs met. Their stealing is
their second chance for a mother, the right mother.

The child fails as a delinquent—fails at school, fails in relationships, "fails" to be an acceptable member of society—in
the attempt to get this deprivation recognized and repaired
(failure in this story means the child not getting what she or he
needs for her or his own optimal development). Success in
Winnicott's account—a radical revision of Freud in the sense
that personal development is privileged over instinctual gratification—means becoming what we have it in ourselves to be.
Where Freud sees, in the title of one of his most remarkable
papers, "Instincts and Their Vicissitudes," Winnicott sees the
struggle for development, what he refers to as "the imaginative
elaboration of physical function," the becoming of the "true
self." And for Winnicott, development depends upon the taking

of second chances, especially whether or not they are seen as such (it is the so-called "true self" that takes and makes second chances, the true self being, for Winnicott, the developing self, the self that carries the child's real potential for growth). It is as though children, in his account, are instinctively and unconsciously masters of the second chance, and masters of the art of the second chance (it requires their being able to make nuisances of themselves, to use symbols to represent what is lacking, to find and appeal to a useful audience). Children "know" the second chance they need and they believe, or hope, that it is possible. "It is an essential feature," Winnicott writes, "that the infant has reached to a capacity to perceive that the cause of the disaster lies in an environmental failure."[14] Indeed, if we want to understand what a second chance is, Winnicott intimates, we need to see how children take them, and take to them, make them and make them out. We need to go back to the first second chances, which in this story are all related to mothering and development.

But in Winnicott's account it should be noted that both the mother and the child can be in need of second chances. Writing of the "mother's indulgence of her infant," reactive to the infant's sense of deprivation, Winnicott suggests that

> Mother-love is often thought of in terms of this indulgence, which in fact is *a therapy in respect of a failure of mother-love.* It is a therapy, a second chance given to mothers who cannot always be expected to succeed in their initial most delicate task of primary love. If the mother does this therapy as a reaction formation arising out of her own complexes, then what she does is called spoiling. In so far as she is able to do it because she sees the necessity for the child's claims to be met, and for the child's compul-

sive greediness to be indulged, then it is a therapy
that is usually successful. Not only the mother, but
the father, and indeed the family, may be involved.[15]

In the last sentence Winnicott clearly wants to take the
heat off the mother. But it is equally clearly intelligently sym-
pathetic to suggest that mothers, too, need second chances faced
with the exorbitant demands of their children (and the exorbitant internal demands they make of themselves to be good-
enough mothers). Without the mother's being able to go on
taking the second chance of indulging her child, having recognized the child's frustration, the child is stranded in her or his
deprivation, and the mother is abandoned to her supposed cruelty and neglect. But what Winnicott wants to stress here is that
although things are bound to go wrong between the mother
and child—and, indeed, between people in any relationship—
everything depends on how things are repaired. That is, in the
belief and confidence in second chances. So by the same token
Winnicott will write elsewhere, in a case history, about a six-
year-old child who "had an acute need to be a baby and to have
a second chance to make use of his mother in a dependent
state."[16] In the second chance the potential in the first chance is
recovered, and realized. This child needed a period of recon-
necting with the mother of whom he had been deprived by the
birth of a sibling. But the second chance can work only if there
was, as it were, something to work with in the first chance—
here, a good-enough mother who could be satisfyingly regressed
to. For Winnicott second chances are possible only if there has
been a first chance, a first chance with perceived potential.

The second chance, then, for Winnicott is reactive to a
failure, and it is full of hope (the possibility of the second chance
is what both inspires and carries hope). It restarts development,
and the implication is that development is something that is

continually in need of restarting (the question for men over fifty, Winnicott apparently once remarked, is whether they want to go on growing). And Winnicott is particularly mindful of just how precarious second chances can be. "Over and over again," he writes in "The Antisocial Tendency," "one sees the moment of hope wasted, or withered, because of mismanagement or intolerance."[17] A moment of hope, a second chance, can age badly, wither into bitterness and regret. For the second chance to work, the child has to have the wherewithal to express her or his predicament—the artfulness, the ingenuity, the confidence—and the environment, the parents, the audience have to be sufficiently attentive and alert. So many such moments of hope are wasted when delinquent behavior is merely punished. Winnicott is alerting us to the misrecognition that is all too often what punishment is, and of how much depends on second chances being recognized as such, and being seen to be required.

Winnicott implies that the growing child has something akin to an instinct for second chances—that just as deprivation is inevitable in life, the second chance is its necessary complement and self-cure. To be frustrated without the possibility of a second chance is to be driven mad; and in Winnicott's account, to be driven mad is to be prevented from sufficiently developing. Freud believes that we also need to learn to live without second chances, and to be duly realistic about what second chances might mean.

Conclusion

To believe in second chances is to run the risk of willful optimism—unless, that is, we imagine that a life can be revised the way a text, or a design, or a plan can be. Second chances are akin to second thoughts, in that they imply a capacity for reconsideration, something to which Shakespeare is acutely attentive in his writing. To believe in second chances is to believe that lives can to some extent be put right, that the future can improve—and improve upon the past—that what has been lost can be recovered. The whole idea of second chances, in other words, confronts us with the vexed questions of what it is realistic for us to hope for and what it is within our power to do to secure the lives we want; second chances are one of the things we can look forward to, even though, as second chances, they challenge us to do something we could not do the first time round. (And we may, of course, be unable to prevent them from being merely deadening repetitions of those first chances we are wanting to revise.) Chances, of course, have to be seen to be taken. And second chances have to be seen to have something that the first chances did not, but seen nevertheless as reminders. (It is because a second chance makes us think of previous options that it becomes, for us, a second chance.) Second chances are always testing our capacity to take our chances, and our capacity to sustain them as the fortunate chances they might be. We may, then, take re-marriage or adopting a child or recovering from a serious ill-ness or an accident as familiar emblems, among many, for the question of second chances, those second chances that make repetition enlivening.

Believing in the possibility of second chances makes us not merely clever animals but redemptive animals, who can res-cue themselves, and be rescued from, whatever is deemed to have gone wrong with their lives; who can recover their poten-tial; who can use time to their advantage. Such a belief reveals us to be creatures who can learn from experience and go on experimenting with what might be best for themselves, crea-tures who know, who can recognize when, through their own conscious or unconscious destructiveness, something has gone really wrong with their lives—when something has failed, or faltered, or collapsed, or been spoiled, or attacked—and have useful and effective ideas (what and whom they can depend upon, or what and who their real resources are about what to do about it, and who can do it). Creatures who are able to repair and restore what they may have broken, or squandered, or sac-rificed. Creatures who can have legitimate and realistic hope for themselves and for others. The idea of second chances, that is to say, both is eminently practical and can be, on occasion, unduly wishful (second chances can seem to make losses re-deemable). We turn to Freud to understand our passion for wish-ing, and indeed for what can count, and for what we can count on, as realistically practical and practicable (the real being that which we cannot wish away). And, as we have suggested, it is to Shakespearean tragedy that we can go to see what a life looks like that is hostile to and cannot conceive of a second chance; and to Shakespeare's comedies and late romances to see what second chances can do for the shape and purpose of a lived life. Indeed, what passes as a first chance in Shakespeare's comedies is always already a second chance. This is what is fully realized in the so-called romances: that unbeknownst to the protagonists, second chances have been coming thick and fast. Freud, of course, would agree that more second chances are available if only we could let ourselves see them or risk them.

To be able to recognize a second chance, and to be able to take it, is to have confidence that the past, even though it may inform everything, predicts or determines nothing with any certainty. Far from there being, as Freud suggested, and many of us experience, a "repetition compulsion"—something that appears to have a life of its own inside us through which we keep putting ourselves in all-too-familiar distressing and deadly situations, and which the psychoanalyst Charles Rycroft defines as "an innate tendency to revert to earlier conditions . . . an innate drive, the death instinct, to return to the inanimate"— the whole idea of second chances implies progress where there was once regression, renewal and revision where there were once compulsion and despair.[1] The second chance is the chance, that is to say, that one may be able to relinquish or use to escape from certain destructive compulsions that have organized one's life. Instead of the seemingly automatic recurrence of traumatic experiences, the spell cast by the trauma is broken; instead of endless regression there are growth and development. From a psychoanalytic point of view, trauma arrests the developmental process, and the innate developmental process itself needs to be given the second chance of a new start. Repetition then becomes not simply more of the same, but an opportunity to innovate and improvise, to do something new or to do something else within the existing constraints. What may have begun, first, as tragedy can become—as in *The Winter's Tale*—romance (or comedy). A catastrophic disillusionment can become—as it cannot in *Othello* or *King Lear*—a more benign recovery of fluency and assurance. Second chances are by definition enlivening and benignly transformative. They are associated with a recovery, a restoration, a coming back to life.

Indeed, it has been part of the confidence of psychoanalysis and many of the other so-called psychological therapies—which themselves, as treatments, promise a second chance for a stalled life—that understanding, and so resolving, our foiled or missed first chances can undo the knots that have preempted our development, and help us get the lives we would prefer. The paralyzing and stultifying repetitions in our lives can be replaced by growth, aliveness, and the shock of the new. As Freud wrote in his earlier, more encouraging days, "A thing which has not been understood inevitably reappears; like an unlaid ghost, it cannot rest until the mystery has been solved and the spell broken."[2] For Freud it is the understanding of psychoanalysis that provides the second chance. What sounds like a second chance here—"the mystery has been solved and the spell broken"—depends upon the understanding of the nature and the preconditions of this mystery, this spell which turns out, Freud intimates, to have been a first chance that was waylaid or misfired or short-circuited, and was radically disabling (the ghost representing the aftereffect of unfinished business). Something went wrong that needed to be righted for things to be able to change. The image is of release and relief. Something, Freud implies, has to be done to the past, to what was too disturbing in the past, which he calls understanding, and which will release the future from the stifling and hypnotic grip of the past (and involve a redescription of what understanding might be). Despite the radical unconscious determinism of our lives that Freud described, he clearly believes, in his commitment to psychoanalytic treatment, that we can have some say in our lives; and this is where the idea of second chances comes in. Where once we were haunted or possessed by something in the past, traumatic events or desires—something that to all intents and purposes, like an addiction, organized our lives and froze time— we are precipitated into an unknown open future. (Shakespeare's comedies and romances, it should be noted, end with gestures toward the future, the romances suggesting that this future will inevitably be limited by time.) And so, by the same token, the second chance promised by psychoanalytic understanding brings with it the fear of a newfound freedom, a more open, less arranged future that the repetition compulsion was a refuge from. This is what Freud would refer to as the "negative therapeutic reaction," the patient's resistance to the treatment and the cure. We should not underestimate, in other words, our fear of second chances, for which Freud's so-called repetition compulsion is an attempted self-cure: the second chance as an invitation we sometimes need to refuse. This is the refusal we find so vividly dramatized in Shakespeare's tragic heroes. The apparent plausibility (and eloquence) of the heroes' self-justifications mask the refusal in them and expose so vividly how well suited self-vindication is to the violence of defensiveness.

The past, one might say, looking back, was full of first chances—of new experiences, of experiments avoided, of opportunities shied away from, of risks not taken, of good things sabotaged and betrayed—that can be described and redescribed: any description has its own second chance, as redescription. In the psychoanalytic project of redescription—a kind of secular alchemy—past losses can be transformed into future gains. What look like first chances, missed chances—even traumas—in retrospect can be the material, the necessary material, out of which second chances are made. Looking back, at least from a psychoanalytic point of view, we can feel as if we did not even make mistakes, or suffer setbacks, so much as we revealed—as in a Freudian slip—conflicting and diverse intentions that might be made good in the future. Our first chances, in this fortifying progress myth—more optimistic and enlivening than the psychoanalytic view is conventionally deemed to be—are what we have to work with. If, that is, we have the desire, or the wherewithal, or the right conversations; if we have the second chance of learning that there are second chances in life. Only those who believe, unlike Othello and Lear, that they can be mistaken—Hamlet and Macbeth are notably capable of the wondering conflict that is self-doubt—and believe they can make reparation and want to do so, and who believe that they have some kind of so-called free will—that they can to some extent be the albeit skeptical authors of their own lives, make experimental choices and enjoy preferences—have what we have learned to call second chances. Second chances, that is to say, test our skepticism.

As we can see in the cruelty and havoc of Shakespeare's tragic heroes, without the possibility of second chances, without the desire for second chances and the confidence that they might exist, we are wholly dependent on luck and circumstance (and narcissism) to achieve the lives we might want. What Freud and his followers add, from a modern perspective, to the cultural conversation dramatized by Shakespeare are formalized, entirely secular explanations of what might usefully be described as the first chances in a (modern) individual's personal development, and what second chances may then be a solution to. To believe in second chances, in short, is to believe, as psychoanalysis does, that some people can change and be changed, and that they can change and be changed in ways they prefer, that our lives can to some extent be compatible with our best intentions for ourselves. And this means that our lives can have an always provisional and occasionally intelligible coherence. That there are discernible and evolving patterns in our lives because character is not fixed or preemptively definable. That what we want for ourselves can be in accord with what we try to make of ourselves, or of what happens to ourselves. That at least some missed opportunities can be restored, that some apparently lost potential can be recognized and realized.

And as both Shakespeare and Freud show us in their very different ways, we create and re-create ourselves in dialogue. Our conversations are always, perhaps inevitably, underwritten by the question of second chances, of what we can do and what is irrevocable, of what we must put up with and what we can alter. (In conversation we consider and reconsider our options.) Conversations that begin in childhood and are always about what is and is not possible between, in the first instance, parents and children. (Childhood could be described as one second chance after another in the ongoing conciliation of competing claims that growing up always involves.) Indeed the psychoanalytic story of child development is all about what prevents and what facilitates the child's taking the chances that each new developmental stage offers. Psychobiological development—growing up—in this account is ideally a series of second chances, the ongoing reworking and revision and elaboration of each prior developmental achievement (think of learning to walk). It is the idea of having a second chance at something ushering in a sense of redeemable and recurring opportunity, and of potential competence. Without the notion of a second chance promoted by the adults (it is of course the adults who have to initiate the child into this process, and contain the child's anxiety), the child will keep feeling defeated and stuck. This is why it is useful, for example, to describe walking, after crawling, as a second chance for the child's independent mobility, or puberty as the second chance for the passionate desires and longings of childhood, and so on and on until, apparently, the chance of there being second chances begins to run out (there is a stage, presumably, in everyone's life, at which second chances seem to be impossible or irrelevant). And by describing these by-now familiar early developmental stages as also versions of second chances, we can describe the first chances to which they refer as rehearsals; even though, of course, the rehearsals of childhood are likely to be rehearsals for what will ultimately be unrehearsed and unrehearsable, the uncertainties and unpredictabilities of adult life. Without the idea of second chances, individual development—and, indeed, the story of a life—becomes an ordeal of compliance to the supposedly irreversible. It is the difference between having a fate and having a choice. Or of having a life supposedly driven by unconscious desire and a life inspired by the dialogue between unconscious desire and conscious intention.

In the light of the idea of the second chance, the first chances in our lives begin to look like rehearsals, our unknowing preparation for future opportunities. Our early relationships with our parents and siblings are, say, akin to rehearsals for relationships outside the family; our first loves, rehearsals for later loves. What the idea of second chances adds to the idea of development is the idea of significant and formative revisions in a life, as opposed to and alongside an unfolding ineluctable organic life cycle. Once we describe something as a second chance we have created a more or less self-authored coherent narrative history of our lives. Once the idea of the second chance is in play, our lives cease to be merely episodic or overdetermined by the past. Our lives become also something we make, rather than simply something we undergo, or suffer. The question then becomes, What has to happen, what do people have to do, to spoil their belief in, their assumption of there being, second chances, an assumption, ideally, coming partly from the cumulative second chances of childhood? Or what might be the preconditions—cultural, historical, personal—for the confident assumption that at least in some areas of our lives, preferably the areas of our lives that matter most to us, second chances are possible?

From the more personal point of view of psychoanalytic developmental theory it has long been stressed—initially from observation of mothers and infants, and later from psychotherapy with children—that though inevitably things go wrong between mothers and their infants, and between parents and children (between people), what really matters is how, and whether, things are repaired. Reparation is the constitutive second chance for relationships after the unavoidable mismatches, misrecognitions, and inattentions that disrupt and rupture them in the first place. Whether it is a passive hope—the psychoanalyst Donald Meltzer once remarked that when you have an argument with someone you love you have to wait and see whether the person becomes lovable to you again—or the more active making of amends, it is the mending that matters. In this account, among the preconditions for a belief in second chances would be the cumulative experience, beginning in childhood, of good-enough reparation after disarming and disturbing conflict.

In Shakespeare's plays—as in most dramas, and all psychoanalytic treatments—the story begins with something going wrong; and in the Shakespearean tragedies we have seen that, unlike the late romances, repair is preempted and displaced by revenge, revenge—in the Freudian account, the repetition compulsion at its most extreme and destructive—seeming to be the alternative to, the refusal of, reparation. The escalation of violence preferred to the understanding of what might have prompted it, revenge always forecloses the possibility of new experience, of discovery. Should we choose revenge, then, which is always more of the same, or a second chance which is not? What is it that can be more alluring, more tempting, more satisfying about revenge, what can abolish second, more conciliatory thoughts?

If conflict between people is taken to be unavoidable—taken
to be the point, not the problem—as it is in Shakespearean
drama and Freudian psychoanalysis, then the question will
always be, What, if any, kind of second chance can come out of
any given conflict? Or, to put it differently, What is the desire
for a life without second chances a desire for?

Notes

Introduction

1. John Milton, *Paradise Lost,* in Milton, *Complete Poems and Major Prose,* ed. Merritt Y. Hughes (Indianapolis: Odyssey Press, 1957), 12.587.

2. Homer, *The Odyssey,* trans. Robert Fagles (New York: Viking, 1996), 11.548–52, 555–58.

3. Homer, *The Odyssey,* 13:329–31.

4. Adam Phillips, *Missing Out: In Praise of the Unlived Life* (New York: Farrar, Straus and Giroux, 2013).

5. John Milton, *The Divorce Tracts of John Milton: Texts and Contexts,* ed. Sara J. van den Berg and W. Scott Howard (Pittsburgh: Duquesne University Press, 2010), p. 77.

6. William Shakespeare, *Hamlet,* 5.2.294–95, 290, 285–86, in *The Norton Shakespeare,* 3rd ed., ed. Stephen Greenblatt et al. (New York: Norton, 2015). Further quotations from the plays of Shakespeare will be from this edition and will be cited by act, scene, and line number.

7. Shakespeare, *Hamlet,* 5.2.328–32.

8. Ben Jonson, *Timber; or, Discoveries,* in *Ben Jonson,* ed. Ian Donaldson (Oxford: Oxford University Press, 1985), p. 541.

9. Michel de Montaigne, "Of Repentance" (1585–88), in *The Complete Essays of Montaigne,* trans. Donald M. Frame (Stanford: Stanford University Press, 1957), p. 615; Montaigne "Of Repenting," 3.2, trans. John Florio (1603), in *Shakespeare's Montaigne: The Florio Translation of the "Essays": A Selection,* ed. Stephen Greenblatt and Peter G. Platt (New York: New York Review Books, 2014), p. 196; Montaigne, "Of the Inconsistency of Our Actions" (1572–74), in *Complete Essays,* p. 240.

10. Montaigne, "Of the Inconsistency of Our Actions," p. 242. This is not at all the case with Shakespeare, who, like Matthias Schwarz, depends on cos-

tume to make up the full force and history of identity. Shakespeare puts his energy into his characters who will then be performed again and again but always in different forms, with different people playing the roles.

11. Shakespeare, *The Tempest*, 5.1.305–8, 313–15.

12. The only significant exception is the villain Antonio, whose failure to experience any change in his character is a clear sign of his unregenerate nature. Even Caliban is transformed.

13. In *The Tempest*, as in *Hamlet*, the explicit invocation of life as story anticipates that the story is coming to an end.

> and so to Naples,
> Where I have hope to see the nuptial
> Of these our dear-belovèd solemnized;
> And thence retire me to my Milan, where
> Every third thought shall be my grave. (5.1.311–14)

The perception that the story makes sense only in retrospect is illuminated by an important passage in Kierkegaard's journal: "It is perfectly true, as philosophers say, that life must be understood backwards. But they forget the other proposition, that it must be lived forwards. And if one thinks over that proposition, it becomes more and more evident that life can never really be understood in time simply because at no particular moment can I find the necessary resting-place from which to understand it—backwards" (quoted in Richard Wollheim, *The Thread of Life* [Cambridge: Cambridge University Press, 1984], p. 162). There are significant reflections on this passage both in Wollheim's book and in an essay by Bernard Williams, "Life as Narrative," *European Journal of Philosophy* 17, no. 2 (2009): 305–14.

14. Shakespeare, *The Tempest*, 3.3.89, 82–84; 5.1.313.

15. Shakespeare, *Hamlet* 1.5.190–91; 3.1.150–51.

16. Shakespeare, *Othello* 5.2.261.

17. Shakespeare, *The Tempest*, 1.2.50, 47; Shakespeare, *A Midsummer Night's Dream*, 3.2.207–8; Shakespeare, *As You Like It*, 1.3.69–72.

18. Shakespeare, *Richard III*, 4.4.168–69 (in *3 Henry VI*, 5.6.53, it is observed ominously that he was born with teeth); 2.4.18–19; Shakespeare, *Coriolanus*, 1.3.56–61.

19. Shakespeare, *A Midsummer Night's Dream*, 3.2.324–25; Shakespeare, *2 Henry IV*, 3.2.276–78; Shakespeare, *Hamlet*, 1.2.141–43 (the fact that there is no trace of this element in Horatio's report is a sign of its inadequacy as a summary of the story of Hamlet's life).

20. Shakespeare, *2 Henry IV*, 3.1.76–82.

21. On occasion, Shakespeare depicts situations in which there is no agency

at all: the lovers in *A Midsummer Night's Dream* whose eyes have been anointed with the love juice, for example, or Leontes in *The Winter's Tale* seized by a paranoid delusion, or the conspirators in *The Tempest*, frozen by Prospero's magic into immobility. But for the most part, even when they are in the grip of inward or outward forces over which they have very little control, Shakespeare's characters deliberate, weigh alternatives, and make decisions. And if we regard those decisions as fated—after all, how much freedom does Macbeth, for all his anguishing about whether or not to kill Duncan, actually have?—our skepticism is not very different from the skepticism we might feel about our own most constrained or overdetermined actions, actions for which we nonetheless hold ourselves responsible or are held responsible by institutions of justice.

22. Shakespeare, *Twelfth Night*, 5.1.391–94; Shakespeare, *The Tempest*, 5.1.48–50, 56–57; E.11–13.

23. Sigmund Freud, "Remembering, Repeating, and Working Through: Further Recommendations on the Technique of Psycho-Analysis II" (1914), in *The Standard Edition of the Complete Psychological Works of Sigmund Freud*, trans. James Strachey, vol. 12: *1911–1913: "The Case of Schreber," "Papers on Technique," and Other Works* (London: Hogarth, 1958), p. 151.

24. Shakespeare, *Measure for Measure*, 2.2.118–24.

25. Shakespeare, *Coriolanus*, 5.3.182–83.

26. Shakespeare, *Romeo and Juliet*, P.12.

1

Shakespeare's First Chance

1. William Shakespeare, *The Comedy of Errors*, 1.2.35–40, in *The Norton Shakespeare*, 3rd ed., ed. Stephen Greenblatt et al. (New York: Norton, 2015). Further quotations from the plays of Shakespeare will be from this edition and will be cited by act, scene, and line number. *King Lear* is quoted from the "Combined Text," based on the Folio with interpolated passages from the First Quarto.

2. Shakespeare, *Pericles, Prince of Tyre*, 5.3.46–47.

3. Shakespeare, *Pericles*, 5.1.81–85.

4. Shakespeare, *The Tempest*, 1.2.50.

5. Shakespeare, *Cymbeline*, 4.2.175–80; 5.5.363–65, 368–69, 369–71.

6. Shakespeare, *The Comedy of Errors*, 5.1.402–4, 407.

7. Shakespeare, *The Comedy of Errors*, 5.1.297–99, 308–11, 312–19.

8. Shakespeare, *The Comedy of Errors*, 5.1.320, 379, 386, 393, 392, 408.

9. Shakespeare, *Twelfth Night*, 3.4.342.

10. Shakespeare, *King Lear*, 1.1.94–95, 98–100.

11. Shakespeare, *As You Like It*, 1.2.144–47, 226; 3.5.81, quoting Christopher Marlowe, *Hero and Leander*, in *Christopher Marlowe: The Complete Poems and Translations*, ed. Stephen Orgel (New York: Penguin, 2007), 1:176.

12. Shakespeare, *Twelfth Night*, 1.5.276–80; Shakespeare, *The Tempest*, 1.2.439–40, 449.

13. Shakespeare, *The Tempest*, 1.2.417; Shakespeare, *Romeo and Juliet*, 2.1.7–10, 66–67.

14. Shakespeare, *The Tempest*, 5.1.183–84; Shakespeare, *As You Like It*, 4.1.82–94, 179–82.

15. Shakespeare, *Romeo and Juliet*, 2.1.43.

16. Shakespeare, *A Midsummer Night's Dream*, 1.1.94–95.

17. Shakespeare, *A Midsummer Night's Dream*, 4.1.185–88.

18. Shakespeare, *A Midsummer Night's Dream*, 1.1.47, 41, 42–44.

19. Shakespeare, *As You Like It*, 5.4.107–8, 99–101, 155–56.

20. Shakespeare, *Hamlet*, 4.4.40; Shakespeare, *Twelfth Night*, 5.1.216, 220–21, 222, 232–38.

21. Shakespeare, *Twelfth Night*, 5.1.249–53, 311–13.

22. Shakespeare, *As You Like It*, 5.4.100–101.

23. Shakespeare, *The Comedy of Errors*, 5.1.419–20, 426–27.

24. Shakespeare, *Twelfth Night*, 1.2.7; 2.2.32, 39–40; 2.4.111–12.

25. Shakespeare, *Twelfth Night*, 5.1.369–70; 2.2.39–40.

26. Shakespeare, *The Comedy of Errors*, 5.1.320.

27. Shakespeare, *The Tempest*, 1.2.44–45.

28. Shakespeare, *Pericles*, 5.1.25–26.

29. Shakespeare, *Pericles*, 5.1.20–22; Shakespeare, *As You Like It*, 5.4.151.

30. Shakespeare, *A Midsummer Night's Dream*, 5.1.409–14.

2

No Second Chances

1. William Shakespeare, *Macbeth*, 5.3.23, in *The Norton Shakespeare*, 3rd ed., ed. Stephen Greenblatt et al. (New York: Norton, 2015). Further quotations from the plays of Shakespeare will be from this edition and will be cited by act, scene, and line number. *King Lear* is quoted from the "Combined Text," based on the Folio with interpolated passages from the First Quarto.

2. Shakespeare, *Macbeth*, 1.7.1–2, 9–10, 31.

3. Shakespeare, *Macbeth*, 1.7.39–41, 45–47, 49, 54–59, 59, 79–80.

4. Shakespeare, *Macbeth*, 1.3.22, 137–38, 141–44.

5. Shakespeare, *Macbeth*, 1.3.51, 11, 31; 2.1.36, 38.

6. Shakespeare, *Macbeth*, 2.1.62.

7. Shakespeare, *Macbeth*, 2.2.109; 3.4.138–40.

8. Shakespeare, *Macbeth*, 5.1.19, 26–28.

9. Shakespeare, *Julius Caesar*, 1.1.24; 2.2.3, 56.

10. Shakespeare, *Julius Caesar*, 2.3.12; 3.1.6–10.

11. Shakespeare, *King Lear*, 1.1.147–52.

12. Shakespeare, *King Lear*, 1.1.90–91, 120–21, 168.

13. Shakespeare, *King Lear*, 1.1.49, 53–56, 70–74.

14. Shakespeare, *King Lear*, 1.1.97–101.1.

15. Shakespeare, *King Lear*, 1.1.37.

16. Shakespeare, *King Lear*, 1.5.20; 2.4.275–77.

17. Shakespeare, *King Lear*, 2.4.139, 141–43; Shakespeare, *As You Like It*, 2.7.165–66; Shakespeare, *King Lear*, 4.6.104.

18. Shakespeare, *King Lear*, 4.7.56–60, 65–67.

19. Shakespeare, *King Lear*, 5.3.8–17.

20. Shakespeare, *King Lear*, 5.3.233–35, 239.

21. Shakespeare, *King Lear*, 5.3.239–41.

22. Shakespeare, *King Lear*, 5.3.283–84, 286–87; 5.3.244.

23. Shakespeare, *King Lear*, 1.1.288–89; 5.3.300.

24. Shakespeare, *Othello*, 1.3.291; 3.3.144–47, 149–50, 163, 217–18, 243–44.

25. Shakespeare, *Othello*, 4.1.168–69, 172–75.

26. Shakespeare, *Othello*, 3.3.87–88; 4.2.80; 4.3.17–20.

27. Shakespeare, *Othello*, 4.1.185, 186–87, 188.

28. Shakespeare, *Othello*, 5.2.7–13.

29. Shakespeare, *Othello*, 5.2.122.

30. Shakespeare, *Hamlet*, 5.2.306–7; 3.1.78–79; Shakespeare, *Othello*, 5.2.268–69, 271–74.

3

Second Chances and Delinquency

1. William Shakespeare, *1 Henry IV*, 1.1.84; 3.2.36–38, in *The Norton Shakespeare*, 3rd ed., ed. Stephen Greenblatt et al. (New York: Norton, 2015). Further quotations from the plays of Shakespeare will be from this edition and will be cited by act, scene, and line number.

2. Shakespeare, *1 Henry IV*, 3.2.87.

3. Shakespeare, *1 Henry IV*, 1.2.14, 124; 2.4.13–17.

4. Shakespeare, *1 Henry IV*, 1.2.50–51.

5. Shakespeare, *1 Henry IV*, 1.2.170, 173, 177–78.

6. Shakespeare, *Hamlet*, 3.1.152.

7. Shakespeare, *1 Henry IV*, 1.2.134–35.

8. Shakespeare, *1 Henry IV*, 4.2.59–60.

9. Shakespeare, *2 Henry IV*, 1.2.150, 183–84.

10. Shakespeare, *2 Henry IV*, 1.2.6–8, 8–9.

11. Shakespeare, *2 Henry IV*, 4.2.80–81, 81–82.

12. Shakespeare, *2 Henry IV*, 4.2.89–92, 106–10.

13. Shakespeare, *Richard II*, 5.6.39–40, 50.

14. Shakespeare, *2 Henry IV*, 4.3.313–14.

15. Shakespeare, *1 Henry IV*, 1.2.80–84, 91–92; 2.4.374–79.

16. Shakespeare, *1 Henry IV*, 2.4.408–11, 435–37, 438.

17. Shakespeare, *1 Henry IV*, 1.2.170–71.

18. Shakespeare, *1 Henry IV*, 5.3.52; Shakespeare, *2 Henry IV*, 5.5.24.

19. Shakespeare, *1 Henry IV*, 1.2.183–92.

20. Shakespeare, *2 Henry IV*, 5.2.122–28, 132.

21. Shakespeare, *Henry V*, 2.1.82; Shakespeare, *2 Henry IV*, 5.5.75, 93.

22. Shakespeare, *1 Henry IV*, 1.2.187.

23. Shakespeare, *Antony and Cleopatra*, 1.4.25–26, 18–21, 17.

24. Shakespeare, *Antony and Cleopatra*, 1.2.115–16, 127, 130, 134; 1.3.86.

25. Shakespeare, *Antony and Cleopatra*, 1.1.25–26, 34–35, 47–48.

26. Plutarch, *The Life of Marcus Antonius*, trans. Thomas North (1579), in *Shakespeare's Plutarch*, vol. 2: *The Main Sources of "Antony and Cleopatra" and of "Coriolanus,"* ed. C. F. Tucker Brooke (New York: Duffield, 1909), p. 38; Shakespeare, *Antony and Cleopatra*, 2.2.206–9.

27. Shakespeare, *Antony and Cleopatra*, 1.3.3–6, 10.

28. Shakespeare, *Antony and Cleopatra*, 1.2.128–29; 2.3.39; 3.10.17–20.

29. Shakespeare, *Antony and Cleopatra*, 3.10.21–23; 3.11.7; 3.10.91; 3.13.117–21, 184, 191–92.

30. Shakespeare, *Antony and Cleopatra*, 3.3.187–88.

31. Shakespeare, *Antony and Cleopatra*, 4.14.99–101; 4.15.19–22.

32. Shakespeare, *Antony and Cleopatra*, 5.2.283.

4
Shakespeare's Second Chance

1. William Shakespeare, *The Winter's Tale*, 3.2.141–42, in *The Norton Shakespeare*, 3rd ed., ed. Stephen Greenblatt et al. (New York: Norton, 2015). Further quotations from the plays of Shakespeare will be from this edition and

will be cited by act, scene, and line number. *King Lear* is quoted from the "Combined Text," based on the Folio with interpolated passages from the First Quarto.

2. Robert Greene, *Greene's Groatworth of Wit*, in E. K. Chambers, *William Shakespeare*, 2 vols. (Oxford: Clarendon, 1930), vol. 2, p. 188.

3. Shakespeare, *The Winter's Tale*, 1.1.19–21; 1.2.27, 108–11.

4. Shakespeare, *The Winter's Tale*, 1.2.67–69.

5. Shakespeare, *The Winter's Tale*, 2.1.40–46, 46.

6. Shakespeare, *The Winter's Tale*, 1.2.273, 296–98, 276–78, 304–6; 2.1.89, 90, 94; 1.2.299–301.

7. Shakespeare, *The Winter's Tale*, 1.2.138–47; 3.2.78–79, 80.

8. Shakespeare, *The Winter's Tale*, 1.2.325–26, 327–32.

9. Shakespeare, *The Winter's Tale*, 1.2.424–29, 292–96.

10. Shakespeare, *The Winter's Tale*, 2.3.4–6, 7–9.

11. Shakespeare, *The Winter's Tale*, 2.3.1, 1–2.

12. Sigmund Freud, "Remembering, Repeating and Working-Through: Further Recommendations on the Technique of Psycho-Analysis II" (1914), in *The Standard Edition of the Complete Psychological Works of Sigmund Freud*, trans. James Strachey, vol. 12: *1911–1913: "The Case of Schreber," "Papers on Technique" and Other Works* (London: Hogarth, 1958), p. 151; Freud, *Beyond the Pleasure Principle* (1920), in *Standard Edition*, vol. 18: *1920–1922: "Beyond the Pleasure Principle," "Group Psychology" and Other Works* (London: Hogarth, 1955).

13. Shakespeare, *The Winter's Tale*, 1.2.325–26.

14. Jean Laplanche, *Life and Death in Psychoanalysis*, trans. Jeffrey Mehlman (Baltimore: Johns Hopkins University Press, 1976), p. 47.

15. Shakespeare, *The Winter's Tale*, 2.3.13–17.

16. Shakespeare, *The Winter's Tale*, 2.1.57–59.

17. Shakespeare, *The Winter's Tale*, 3.2.130–33.

18. Shakespeare, *The Winter's Tale*, 3.3.57.

19. Shakespeare, *The Winter's Tale*, 5.2.26–27.

20. Shakespeare, *1 Henry IV*, 1.2.192.

21. Shakespeare, *King Lear*, 1.1.231–32; Shakespeare, *The Winter's Tale*, 2.3.133–34, 137–40, 177, 183–84.

22. Robert Greene, *Pandosto, The Triumph of Time*, in Shakespeare, *The Winter's Tale*, ed. John Pitcher (London: Arden Shakespeare, 2010), p. 408; Shakespeare, *The Winter's Tale (Norton Shakespeare)*, 3.2.132–33.

23. Greene, *Pandosto*, pp. 444, 445.

24. Shakespeare, *The Winter's Tale*, 5.1.223–26.

25. Shakespeare, *The Winter's Tale*, 5.1.226–27.

26. Shakespeare, *The Winter's Tale*, 3.2.147, 152–54.

27. Shakespeare, *The Winter's Tale*, 3.2.231–35, 235–39.

28. Shakespeare, *The Winter's Tale*, 2.1.109–10, 112–13; 3.2.91, 105–6.

29. Shakespeare, *The Winter's Tale*, 4.1.19, 17.

30. Shakespeare, *The Winter's Tale*, 5.1.1–4, 27.

31. Shakespeare, *The Winter's Tale*, 5.1.6–9.

32. Shakespeare, *The Winter's Tale*, 5.1.15–17.

33. Shakespeare, *The Winter's Tale*, 5.1.23–24.

34. Shakespeare, *The Winter's Tale*, 3.3.62.

35. Shakespeare, *The Winter's Tale*, 4.3.25, 1–4, 23.

36. Shakespeare, *The Winter's Tale*, 3.3.132–33; 5.1.41.

37. Shakespeare, *The Winter's Tale*, 5.3.94–95, 99–100; 4.1.19; 3.2.91; 5.3.102–3; 4.3.4.

38. Shakespeare, *The Winter's Tale*, 5.3.109, 112–13.

39. Shakespeare, *The Winter's Tale*, 5.3.113, 114–15; 5.2.98.

40. Shakespeare, *The Winter's Tale*, 1.1.34–35.

41. Shakespeare, *The Winter's Tale*, 5.2.48.

42. Shakespeare, *The Winter's Tale*, 5.3.28–29, 34.

43. Shakespeare, *The Winter's Tale*, 5.3.154–55.

44. Shakespeare, *The Winter's Tale*, 5.3.147–49; 1.2.182–84.

45. Shakespeare, *The Winter's Tale*, 5.3.123–28.

46. Shakespeare, *The Winter's Tale*, 5.3.128–30.

47. Shakespeare, *The Winter's Tale*, 2.2.45–46.

48. Shakespeare, *The Winter's Tale*, 3.3.103–4.

49. Shakespeare, *The Winter's Tale*, 2.2.61.

50. Shakespeare, *The Winter's Tale*, 5.2.26–27; 5.3.110–11.

5

Come Again

1. William Shakespeare, *1 Henry IV*, 1.2.192, in *The Norton Shakespeare*, 3rd ed., ed. Stephen Greenblatt et al. (New York: Norton, 2015).

2. Sigmund Freud, "Family Romances" (1909), in *The Standard Edition of the Complete Psychological Works of Sigmund Freud*, trans. James Strachey, vol. 9: *1906–1908: Jensen's "Gradiva" and Other Works* (London: Hogarth, 1955), pp. 237–39.

3. Richard Ford, *The Sportswriter* (New York: Vintage, 1995), p. 131.

4. Oscar Wilde, *De Profundis* (New York: Modern Library, 1926), p. 61.

5. D. W. Winnicott, *Playing and Reality* (London: Tavistock, 1971), p. 14.

6. Winnicott, *Playing and Reality*, p. 115.

6
Remembering Second Chances

1. Stanley Cavell, *Pursuits of Happiness: The Hollywood Comedy of Re-marriage* (Cambridge: Harvard University Press, 1981).

2. Masud Khan, "The Concept of Cumulative Trauma," in Khan, *The Privacy of the Self* (London: Hogarth, 1974), chap. 3.

3. Sigmund Freud, *The Ego and the Id* (1923), in *The Standard Edition of the Complete Psychological Works of Sigmund Freud,* trans. James Strachey, vol. 19: *1923–1925: "The Ego and the Id" and Other Works* (London: Hogarth, 1961), p. 49.

4. Sigmund Freud, "Analysis Terminable and Interminable" (1937), in *Standard Edition,* vol. 23: *1937–1939: "Moses and Monotheism," "An Outline of Psychoanalysis," and Other Works* (London: Hogarth, 1964), p. 238.

5. Khan, *The Privacy of the Self,* p. 97.

6. D. W. Winnicott, *Playing and Reality* (London: Tavistock, 1971), p. 2.

7. Roger Money-Kyrle, "The Remote Consequences of Psycho-analysis on Individual, Social and Instinctive Behavior" (1931), in *The Collected Papers of Roger Money-Kyrle,* ed. Donald Meltzer and Edna O'Shaughnessy (London: Clunie, 1978), p. 61.

8. Jean Laplanche and Jean-Bertrand Pontalis, *The Language of Psycho-analysis,* trans. Donald Nicholson-Smith (London: Hogarth, 1973), p. 395.

9. See Jean Laplanche, *Life and Death in Psychoanalysis,* trans. Jeffrey Mehlman (Baltimore: Johns Hopkins University Press, 1976).

10. Sigmund Freud, "The Psychotherapy of Hysteria" (1895), in *Standard Edition,* vol. 2: *1893–1895: Studies on Hysteria* (London: Hogarth, 1955), p. 305.

11. Marcel Proust, *Swann's Way,* trans. C. K. Scott Moncrieff and Terence Kilmartin (New York: Modern Library, 2003), p. 60.

12. Proust, *Swann's Way,* p. 59.

13. Proust, *Swann's Way,* pp. 59–60.

14. Proust, *Swann's Way,* p. 11.

7
Second Chances

1. Franz Kafka, "Leopards in the Temple," in Kafka, *Parables and Paradoxes* (New York: Schocken, 1961), p. 93.

2. See Robert Stoller, *Perversion: The Erotic Form of Hatred* (New York: Routledge, 1975), p. 59.

3. Jean-Paul Sartre, *Mallarmé; or, The Poet of Nothingness*, trans. Ernest Sturm (University Park: Pennsylvania State University Press, 1988), p. 145.

4. Alasdair MacIntyre, *Dependent Rational Animals: Why Human Beings Need the Virtues* (Chicago: Open Court, 1999).

5. Sigmund Freud, "Remembering, Repeating, and Working-Through: Further Recommendations on the Technique of Psycho-Analysis II" (1914), in *The Standard Edition of the Complete Psychological Works of Sigmund Freud*, trans. James Strachey, vol. 12: *1911–1913: "The Case of Schreber," "Papers on Technique," and Other Works* (London: Hogarth, 1958), pp. 145–56; D. W. Winnicott, *Playing and Reality* (London: Tavistock, 1971).

6. Sigmund Freud, *Beyond the Pleasure Principle* (1920), in *Standard Edition*, vol. 18: *1920–1922: "Beyond the Pleasure Principle," "Group Psychology," and Other Works* (London: Hogarth, 1955), pp. 14–15.

7. Freud, *Beyond the Pleasure Principle*, pp. 16–17.

8. Jean Laplanche and Jean-Bertrand Pontalis, *The Language of Psycho-analysis*, trans. Donald Nicholson-Smith (London: Hogarth, 1973), p. 78.

9. Laplanche and Pontalis, *Language of Psychoanalysis*, p. 80.

10. Marion Milner, *A Life of One's Own* (London: Chatto and Windus, 1936).

11. See *Longman Dictionary of Contemporary English, s.v.* "second chance," ldoceonline.com/dictionary/second-chance.

12. D. W. Winnicott, "The Antisocial Tendency" (1956), in Winnicott, *Deprivation and Delinquency* (London: Tavistock, 1984), p. 123.

13. Winnicott, "The Antisocial Tendency," p. 126.

14. Winnicott, "The Antisocial Tendency," p. 129.

15. Winnicott, "The Antisocial Tendency," p. 128.

16. D. W. Winnicott, "Symptom Tolerance in Paediatrics" (1953), in Winnicott, *Through Paediatrics to Psychoanalysis* (New York, Basic, 1975), p. 113.

17. Winnicott, "The Antisocial Tendency," p. 123.

Conclusion

1. Charles Rycroft, *A Critical Dictionary of Psychoanalysis* (New York: Basic, 1968), p. 156.

2. Sigmund Freud, "Analysis of a Phobia in a Five-Year-Old Boy" (1909), in *The Standard Edition of the Complete Psychological Works of Sigmund Freud*, trans. James Strachey, vol. 10: *1909: Two Case Histories* (London: Hogarth, 1955), p. 122.

Acknowledgments

This book originated in an invitation to deliver the Hecht Lectures at Bard College. We are grateful to Bard's president, Leon Botstein, and to Adhaar Noor Desai, Gideon Lester, Debra Pernstein, Marina van Zuylen, and other faculty and staff for their gracious hospitality. Thanks as well to the American Psychoanalytic Association and to the Lunn Lecture of the University of California, Davis, where versions of several of the chapters were presented. We acknowledge a particular debt of gratitude to Jennifer Banks, Matt Bevis, Stanley Coen, Aubrey Everett, Kit Fan, Erica Hanson, Hugh Haughton, Anselm Haverkamp, Susan Laity, Daniela Nieva, Robert Pinsky, Peter Rudnytsky, David Russell, Peter Sacks, Michael Saler, and Richard Wheeler. We owe our deepest thanks to Judith Clark and Ramie Targoff.

Index